# TELEPHONE ASSESSMENT
## with Protocols for Nursing Practice

**MARY PACKARD SCOTT, RN**

Co-Owner and Associate of Nurseline Associates, Inc.
Seattle, Washington

**KATE PARKER PACKARD, RN, MA**

Co-Owner and Associate of Nurseline Associates, Inc.
Seattle, Washington

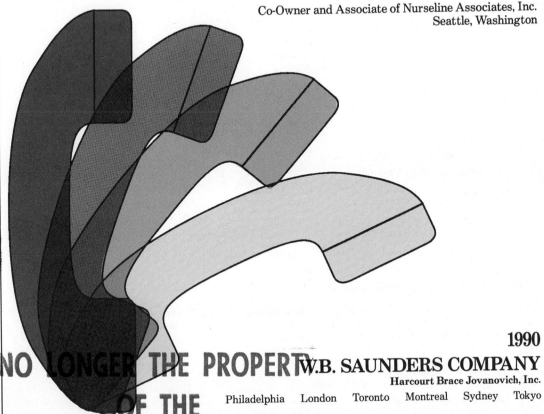

1990

**W.B. SAUNDERS COMPANY**
Harcourt Brace Jovanovich, Inc.

Philadelphia   London   Toronto   Montreal   Sydney   Tokyo

W. B. Saunders Company: The Curtis Center
Independence Square West
Philadelphia, PA   19106-3399

*Editor:*   Michael Brown

*Designer:*   Joan Owen

*Production Manager:*   Pete Faber

*Manuscript Editor:*   Margaret MacKay Eckman

*Illustration Coordinator:*   Walt Verbitski

*Indexer:*   Dena Scher

Telephone Assessment with Protocols for Nursing Practice          ISBN 0-7216-8023-2

Printed in the United States of America
Library of Congress catalog card number 89-10365.


Last digit is the print number:     9   8   7   6   5   4   3   2   1

# Preface

This book evolved in response to two developments in health care: the expansion of nursing practice and the changing relationship between consumers and the health care industry. Health care providers need to market in creative, responsive ways. Consumers need empowerment and access into increasingly complex and costly systems. Nursing has developed a critical link between these two new forces in health care.

Community outreach nursing is a creative approach to marketing health care, both for individual physicians and for institutions, and a service to the community. Nurses are well respected by the public and have expertise in assessing callers' concerns. They are in an excellent position to represent their institutions while assisting the public to make wise, cost-effective health care choices.

Our experience as telephone resource nurses on the forefront of these changes left us with more questions than answers. This book is our attempt to answer some of those questions and to get those answers where they're needed: to the nurses who talk with people on the phone.

This book is a restructuring of the telephone assessment concept. It is a tool to be used for nursing management: not, as has been the case with previous telephone assessment guides, a medical tool used by nurses. It is a strong statement for the value of nursing.

The material in this book was designed for use by experienced professional nurses in a formalized telephone consultation setting. However, it can be adapted for use by any experienced nurse who talks with people on the phone. We have attempted to answer the questions asked by nurses in many areas of practice.

Telephone assessment is mainly communication skills, and experienced nurses will find they know most of this material already. It is important to realize the concepts in this book are not new. They are a restructuring of information good, experienced nurses already know and use all the time. Some of the applications of familiar concepts have changed, and some have been enlarged upon, but very little is new. We have tried to arrange the driest and most familiar material so it doesn't get too boring.

Above all, we have attempted to make this book useful.

Mary Packard Scott
Kate P. Packard

# Acknowledgments

Many of our professional colleagues and friends made suggestions and comments that ultimately altered the character of this book. We are grateful for their comments, and for their support and encouragement.

I, Mary Scott, would like to thank several people whose contributions have been particularly helpful. My parents' support, especially during the spring and summer of 1987, was very important. Amy, my daughter, has philosophically and patiently lived with the disruption of the last few years, and for that I am extremely grateful. Sandra Nickell's assistance with the protocols contributed enormously to their quality, and her encouragement during the last few months has helped maintain my perspective and possibly my sanity.

# Table of Contents

# The Skills of Telephone Assessment

# The Nurse-Caller Interaction

## MUTUAL DECISION MAKING

Several basic assumptions serve as a foundation for the decision making processes explored in this chapter. These essential concepts provide a framework within which all subsequent ideas, concepts, and skills are developed.

### . . . To Facilitate Access

The essential nursing concept in telephone assessment is that of short-term, episodic intervention to facilitate access to the health care system. In contrast to other areas of nursing where longer relationships with patients are fostered, telephone encounters are by their nature short-term and episodic because they are subject to the limits of telephone communication. Although telephone nurses may become well acquainted with frequent callers, telephone encounters lack the intensity and depth provided by face to face communication. What may appear to be a long-term relationship is really a series of individual contacts.

Callers initiating a nursing contact may have very precise ideas of what they want, as in "I just want to know if my toe is broken." It is essential for the nurse to understand and accept the role of a triage provider facilitating access into the health care system to negotiate a satisfactory resolution with a caller whose expectations may be unrealistic.

A thorough grasp of the concept of the nurse as access facilitator, rather than treatment provider, removes the issue of diagnosing disease. Nurses are deeply immersed in medical model thinking, and although this concept may, at first, be difficult to grasp (and difficult to present to callers), it is in the long run liberating as it allows the nurse to become an expert communicator who assists callers in making their own health care decisions.

### The Caller Owns the Problem

For a variety of reasons, including the nurse's sanity and the caller's compliance, nurses must realize that people have very personal reasons for calling, and perhaps hidden agendas. Regardless of a nurse's strong feelings about a given issue, a problem must remain the caller's problem. This idea is central to the view of a telephone encounter as a mutual process between equals. The goal of the nurse is to negotiate a mutually satisfactory solution to the caller's problem. Nurses assist callers' decision making processes; they do not tell people what to do.

Keeping in mind the nurse's goal of assisting callers to make their own health care decisions, it is apparent that the skills needed to ensure that decisions are wise and mutually agreeable are problem solving and negotiating skills. These are communication skills, old-fashioned communication skills; all good nurses have them.

### Building Trust

Quality assessment and caller satisfaction depend on effective communication between the nurse and the caller. Certain techniques foster effective communication by providing an atmosphere of openness and mutual trust, which contributes to information gathering, mutual satisfaction, and compliance by the caller with decisions. A nurse's skill in these techniques not only improves communication, but may also help resolve the problem by providing an atmosphere of acceptance that allows people to think. Sometimes that is all they need.

To begin effective communication, you need a quiet, calm tone of voice and the following:

**Attentiveness:** Let the caller know you are listening by making listening noises. "Oh," "mmm," and "uh-huh" work well. Respond early and genuinely. Stay alert throughout the conversation.

**Acceptance:** Convey to the caller that this is a safe place to say whatever needs to be said. Accept the caller's point of view. Callers need to express their feelings before they can begin to get control of their problems.

**Empathy:** Focus on feelings and convey understanding by paraphrasing: *"Sounds like you feel miserable."* Avoid blocking out emotional areas. (This can be difficult if you don't agree with the caller's view of the situation.) Avoid jargon.

**Equality:** Respect callers. Show a willingness to mutually define and solve the problem: *"I can give you a hand with this." "Together we can think of something." "We can work on this."* Avoid using your medical knowledge to manipulate.
**Genuineness:** Be honest, warm, and straightforward.

The ability to recognize and handle their own feelings, to accept differing values, and to know and accept their own limitations are qualities that help nurses to provide an atmosphere that supports callers.

# THE PROCESS

Keep in mind that the assessment process is a thought process and that the Problem Solving Model presented by this book is just a framework for your own creative processes. It is a pragmatic approach to assist in identifying the stages of a call and to discuss the skills and tools needed at each stage. This particular Problem Solving Model is an adaptation of the Nursing Process and the Crisis Intervention Problem Solving Model.

### Identifying the Problem

The goals of this first stage of the call are to establish a mutually trusting relationship and to identify the problems needing to be addressed. Trust is a function of the healing and nurturing skills already discussed. Using these skills has the added benefit of eliciting information about the caller's concerns.

The most effective information gatherer is silence. The longer you can keep quiet—making only those sounds that let the caller know you're listening—the more information you will be given. Let callers talk themselves out. It may seem, at first, as though calls take longer if you listen without commenting or guiding callers. If, however, they're prevented from fully expressing themselves, callers may not hang up when the call is completed.

Sometimes you need to encourage a caller to talk. You can do this without controlling the caller by using broad, open-ended phrases and by empathizing. *"Tell me more about it." "Explain that to me." "You seem really worried about her."*

Often the initial complaint or problem is not the most crucial, either to the nurse or to the caller. After gathering information, you can help the caller clarify issues and problems by asking more directive, focused questions. *"Which of these symptoms bothers you the most?" "Are you concerned about the cough, or is it just the fever that's worrying you?"*

Rambling, disjointed stories can be clarified by focusing callers in the present. *"It sounds like you've been feeling poorly since 1981; what made you decide to call us today?" "Did something happen recently that's making this worse for you?''* ''*Which of these problems is giving you the most trouble right now?''*

When the caller is finished talking and you think you know what the problem is, summarize it. Do this for both yourself and the caller. *"It seems to me, your concern is not that you feel your son is seriously ill, but that he's going to camp tomorrow. You'll feel better if he's checked before he goes." "It sounds like your main concern is how to get the fever down." "You're worried that your mother's getting so forgetful she may not be safe at home alone."* Be as specific as you can. You will either be right or you will be wrong. If you're right, go on to explore the problem further. If you're wrong, the caller will tell you so. If this happens, be honest about your confusion and ask more questions.

### Exploring the Problem

The goal of this second stage of the call is to collect information pertinent to the problem and to assess its significance. Two types of information tend to present themselves: information about the symptom and information about the emotional context of that symptom. Both need to be explored in order to effectively resolve the problem.

Table 1–1 shows the information needed for a quality assessment, and Table 1–2 shows how to assess a suicidal caller. But how do you get all that information?

**Open-Ended Questions:** Start by asking questions that require the caller to think and talk. Ask questions that begin with who, when, where, how, and tell me. Use any question that requires more than

### Table 1–1. ASSESSMENT PARAMETERS

| The Problem or Symptom | Context |
|---|---|
| Length of time present | Age |
| Course | Chronic disease |
| Description, including: intensity | Accompanying acute illness |
| location | Recent hospitalizations, surgeries |
| quality | Recent injuries |
| character | Medications |
| Accompanying symptoms | Allergies |
| Precipitating factors | Habits |
| Aggravating and ameliorating factors | Occupation |
| Previous episodes and their treatment | Pregnancy |
| Current treatment and its effectiveness | **Coping Mechanisms** |
| Pregnancy | Affect |
| | Anxiety level |
| | Appropriateness of information |
| | Previous calls |

**Table 1–2. THE SUICIDE CALL**

**Remember**
You are not going to stop people from killing themselves if that is what they are determined to do.

Suicidal callers are teetering in a precarious balance. They are not feeling positive about death, but feeling very negative about life. These callers are asking for help, so they are ambivalent about suicide, and the slightest warm caring can tip the balance in favor of life. Remain calm and take your time; this allows the caller to remain calm. These callers need firm direction about what to do.

**Consider Saying the Following to Establish a Relationship**
It sounds like you feel awful. You've called the right place. I can find the help you need. My name is _____. What's yours? Tell me what's going on.

**Questions You Need to Ask to Assess Lethality**
Have you thought about how you could kill yourself?

Do you have the pills, gun, or other means with you? Would you go and put them away while I stay on the line?

Have you been drinking today?

In order to help I need to talk a little about what's been happening to make you feel this badly. Has something happened recently to make you feel this way?

Have you felt this way before?

Has anyone in your family committed suicide?

Where are you? Is anyone there with you? What is the phone number there?

Do you have a counselor? Can you talk to your counselor about how you're feeling?

I want you to talk to someone who is an expert in _____ (caller's problem area). Will you agree not to kill yourself until you talk to them?

Can you agree to call me back if you feel like this again before _____ (the expert) talks to you?

---

a "yes" or "no" response. Be cautious with questions that begin with why. "Why" has a tendency to make people defensive (as in "Why haven't you treated his fever?"). The same information can be elicited by "Have you considered . . . ?" The use of open-ended questions is the single most effective technique for figuring out what's really going on.

**Focusing:** Provide leads for the caller to elaborate on points that seem significant, leaving out those that do not.

**Listen to What's *Not* Being Said:** Emotionally laden subjects are the ones most commonly left out. Identifying these subjects and their attendant emotions is often crucial to the outcome (as in "I'm worried that mother's not safe at home and I feel guilty about sending her to a nursing home").

**Silence:** This is a good way to encourage a caller. There seems to be a universal urge to fill a void.

**Paraphrase:** State in your own words what the caller seems to be saying, particularly about emotions. Restate the basic message as an accuracy check.

**Recognize Ambivalence:** Recognize and help callers recognize when there are strong feelings on both sides of an issue. Identifying ambivalent feelings gives people control of them and is the first step in resolution of conflict.

**"I" Statements:** Stating your own perceptions can create a strong bond between you and the caller. It gives the caller a different point of view. Be careful with this technique. It can be perceived as judgmental and often is, in fact, judgmental.

## The Protocols

It is at this point in the call that you use protocols. Other chapters discuss protocol use in depth, so this is really just an overview, a quick look at timing and function. Protocols are an aid to information gathering. Their purpose is to make certain you don't leave out anything. Rely on your nursing knowledge and communication skills to assess callers' problems. Turn to your protocols only *after* you are satisfied that you have elicited everything you can about the problem. Assessment is a thought process, not a protocol following process; using a protocol too early can cause you to assess inaccurately.

As you assess callers' problems, the temptation to think in terms of diagnoses may arise. It is easy for nurses, because of their extensive knowledge and their familiarity with the diagnostic model, to slip into diagnosing callers' symptoms. This is, after all, what many callers expect when they call a nurse. Do "Does it sound like I have the flu?" and "Tell me if I have what's going around" sound familiar?

Instead of relying on diagnoses, learn to think in terms of nursing assessment, nursing management, and triage. Avoiding the temptation to diagnose requires practice and a conscious, determined focus on improving listening and assessing skills. As you refine these skills, diagnosing ceases to be an issue.

When you avoid diagnosing, you avoid the question "What's wrong with this caller?" The question becomes "What's going on with this caller?"—a broader and more nursing-amenable question. When you know what's going on, it is easy to work within the structure of the protocols to determine how to best handle the problem.

Occasionally, callers resist answering "all those questions." To gain their support and make problem solving a mutual process, these callers need to know what you're doing. Explain it to them. Tell them that you need all the information that can possibly have a bearing on their situation and that you're consulting a book to be sure you don't miss anything.

## Exploring Solutions

The goal of this third stage of the call is to agree on a plan of action.

By now the nurse knows the triage category of the symptoms and must work out a mutually satisfactory solution within that triage category. For instance, a caller with problems and associated symptoms falling into the Assess for Immediate Referral category has several options. Among them are going to the doctor if the doctor is in the office, going to a nearby hospital emergency department or urgent care clinic, and perhaps going to a public health clinic.

It is up to the nurse to assist the caller in deciding which option is most appropriate. Continued assessment of the emotional component and context will assist in this process. What resources does the caller have? How much money? What ability to cope with the situation? What attitudes toward potential solutions? What has already been tried? Frequently all that's needed is permission from the nurse for a caller to take action.

## Home Care and Teaching

There are frequent circumstances when home care or teaching is appropriate, when home care is more appropriate than medical evaluation, when home care and teaching are appropriate until a caller is evaluated, and when teaching will help a caller solve the problem. Now is the time for the possibility of home care to be explored. Negotiate home care and teaching solutions in the same manner as other solutions, keeping in mind the emotional component and context.

Occasionally, callers will request advice or directions in the use of some form of home care not contained in the protocols. This can present a problem, as you need to address callers' concerns without advising them to do something outside the scope of your protocols. The use of ibuprofen for fever is a good example. You need to be frank with callers about this kind of issue. You might say, "*I know the manufacturers are suggesting this drug for fevers, but my guidelines do not, so I can't advise you to use it. I think you'd do better with aspirin or acetaminophen.*" People don't seem to have trouble with this approach, and it presents an excellent teaching opportunity.

## Medication Advice

The issue of when and how to advise a caller in the use of medication can be a tricky one. Everyone seems to agree that it's a necessary and appropriate nursing function, but there are no universal guidelines at this time. The question of whether or not a telephone advice nurse (RN) could advise a caller to use an over-the-counter drug was asked of the Washington State Board of Nursing. The answer was yes. The nurse will be held to the same standards as in any other area of practice. The reasoning was that anyone can advise a person to use an over-the-counter medication (their grandmother, their neighbor, their plumber). The nurse will simply be held to nursing standards. RNs who are not nurse practitioners licensed to prescribe can never advise the use of prescription drugs. This does not, however, preclude *teaching* about prescription drugs, which is a legitimate nursing function.

A reasonable guideline for the nurse dealing with symptomatic

**Table 1–3. MEDICATION REVIEW**

The following are to be discussed with all callers before advising the use of any medication:

The presence of *chronic disease*, significant *medical problems*, or *recent surgery*

Present *medications*

Use of *similar medications* in the past

*Allergies*

The possibility of *pregnancy*

callers and the question of over-the-counter drugs is to use the same judgment and exercise the same precautions as in any other nursing situation. Stay within protocol parameters. Know your medications: doses, side effects, cautions, and contraindications. (All the protocols in the world won't protect you if you advise someone with an ulcer to take aspirin.) Avoid advising callers to take multiple ingredient medications. Don't advise medication for pregnant women, infants, people with chronic illness, or those on multiple prescription drugs. Avoid advising callers to take medicines they've never had before. (Again, this is a guideline. Many experienced nurses are comfortable telling parents to treat their childrens' elevated temperatures with acetaminophen and telling women with menstrual cramps about ibuprofen, even if callers have never used these medications before.)

Table 1–3 discusses the medication review. These are the assessments you must make before advising a caller to use a medication.

## Skills

There are two types of communication skills required at this point: teaching skills and negotiating skills. They are both necessary for effective resolution of callers' problems and are often used together.

The guidelines for teaching over the phone are relatively straightforward. Keep instructions as simple as possible. Give only instructions you are sure the caller can understand. If instructions are complex (home care of children with fevers, for example, is very complex), divide the instructions into small, easily understood steps and have the caller write them down. Sometimes it's a good idea to have callers repeat instructions back to you. Asking callers to repeat what you've told them can be perceived as condescending, however, so reserve this technique for complicated or confusing instructions and explain why you're asking. "*That was a lot of information to get at one time. Do you want to repeat it back to me?*" "*Those were pretty complicated instructions. Will you read them back to me so we can be sure we didn't miss anything?*" Encourage callers to ask questions about their instructions. Being as specific as you can will help elicit specific concerns. "*Do you have any questions about the dose of acetaminophen for each child?*

*About how frequently to give it? About what to do if the fever doesn't go below 103°F.?"*

Occasionally, if instructions are particularly complex (fever, again, is a good example), you may get the best comprehension by having the caller complete part of their instructions (undress the child and give acetaminophen) and then call you back (for instructions on bathing and repeat doses of acetaminophen). This technique has a way of decreasing anxiety because it gives the caller some immediate control over the problem. It also clearly defines home care as a series of individual steps, making it easier to repeat in the future.

The main technique used when exploring solutions is that of persuasion or negotiation. When callers don't want to do what's necessary to resolve a problem, it usually means they have not been listened to adequately. Go back to the techniques used earlier in the call; use nurturing skills, ask open-ended questions, and explore why the caller won't do what's needed to resolve a problem. Discuss the caller's expectations and take them into account. Sometimes you need to be quite frank. *"There is no way I can tell over the phone whether or not your foot is broken. Is there some other way I can help you with this?"* Don't be afraid to be creative and negotiate unusual solutions.

### Assessing Ability to Follow Through

The goals of the final stage of the call are to assure that the solution identified at the third stage of the call can and will be carried out and to identify an alternative plan.

Remember, the quality of your communication will determine your success with callers. If throughout the conversation you adhere to principles of good communication, callers will be open and forthright and their needs will be clear. The solutions you negotiate will be carried out.

There are, however, a few techniques you can use to increase compliance. Giving callers feedback about information they have given can help you arrive at mutually agreeable solutions. If you have doubts about the ability of callers to follow through, ask them if they can comply. Be specific about what you think might interfere with compliance. Ask callers if they have objections to solutions or instructions. "How does this sound to you?" works well. Continue to use nurturing skills; show interest in the caller rather than the problem. If you encounter ambivalence, use open-ended questions, clarify, and focus on the problem until you have agreement on a plan of action.

As a safeguard for callers who are unable to follow through (maybe their car won't start or their doctor moved away), identify an alternative plan. Usually, "Call me back if . . ." is fine, but sometimes a more specific plan presents itself quite clearly. *"If your car doesn't start again, you're going to call your sister for a ride to the doctor. Is that right?"* This technique also serves as protection for the nurse in the event home care doesn't work as planned, or in the event the assessment was inaccurate or incomplete. If rapport with callers is good, they will call back if that option is made available to them.

### How Much Do You Do for Callers? How Much Do They Do for Themselves?

Up to this point, the emphasis has been placed on putting the caller's problem where it belongs—with the caller. This is appropriate. The fact remains, however, that there are people who simply seem unable to act.

There are many reasons for the inability to act on one's own behalf. Since they are often impossible to uncover, the best you can do is realize that the caller is unable to act. Some clues that this is occurring include ambivalence that can't be worked through, a profound lack of resources on the part of the caller (language barriers, lack of education, lack of support), and multifaceted, serious problems for which the health care system offers nothing but barriers. ("My four year old has been sexually assaulted at the day-care center. Child Protective Services referred us to the Sexual Assault Center in my county, but they don't see children. The Sexual Assault Center that sees children won't see her because we don't live in their county.") For these people, consider advocacy. Make calls, ask around, find someone to give them a hand. Many agencies will bend rules when problems are presented by a professional, when they would never consider doing so for callers themselves. Consider making appointments if you're convinced the caller needs very firm direction.

For more routine kinds of problems, like the need to call the Poison Control Center or activate the Emergency Medical System, use teaching and negotiating skills to encourage callers to act in their own behalf. Explain why these agencies would rather talk to the person with the problem than to you. Make arrangements with the caller to call back at a specified time "to check on things" instead.

# Tools 2

Effective acquisition and dispersal of information is a crucial component of any community outreach service. The kinds of information you need to manage fall roughly into four categories: community resources, physician referral, professional backup, and reference material.

## COMMUNITY RESOURCES

A file of community agencies, their phone numbers, and a brief description of their services is essential to you. Keep the amount of specific information in this file to a minimum because the funding and consequently the specifics of these agencies changes frequently. Even the phone numbers change frequently. Cross-referencing every agency as extensively as possible is the key to making this file work. A rotary file works well for this purpose.

When suggesting to callers that a particular agency may be able to help them, keep specifics to a minimum. Since public agencies frequently change their guidelines, eventually you will be wrong if you tell callers what is provided by individual agencies. A more effective approach is to provide callers with several names and phone numbers and the option, "Call me back if . . . ." After a while, it will become obvious which agencies really work for the community and which are bureaucratic mazes. Tables 2–1 and 2–2 give sample lists of community resources and cross-references.

## PHYSICIAN REFERRAL

The specifics of an individual facility's physician referral service are frequently as much political as professional, and they vary a great deal from one service to another. Certain procedures and concerns are

**13**

## Table 2–1. SAMPLE LIST OF COMMUNITY RESOURCES

| | |
|---|---|
| Abortion services | Low income housing |
| Acupuncturists | Medic Alert Foundation |
| Adoption services | Medical subspecialists |
| AIDS support services | Medical supply rental services |
| Alcohol treatment services | Mental health agencies |
| American Cancer Society | Minority services |
| American Heart Association | Nursing homes |
| American Lung Association | Nutrition services |
| American Red Cross | Pharmacies, with hours |
| Child care | Planned Parenthood |
| Child protection agencies | Podiatrists |
| Chiropractors | Poison Control Center |
| Crisis intervention services | Police departments |
| Dental clinics | Public health agencies |
| Dentists | Retirement centers |
| Detoxification centers | Senior services |
| Drug abuse services | Sexual assault centers |
| Easter Seal Society | Sexually transmitted disease clinics |
| Eating disorder services | Speech and hearing services |
| Educational resources | Sports medicine clinics |
| Environmental Protection Agency | Support groups |
| Fire departments | Transportation |
| Food banks | United Way |
| Food and Drug Administration | Urgent care centers |
| Gay support services | Weight control clinics |
| Home health services | Women's health care centers |
| Hospitals | Youth services |
| La Leche League | YMCA |
| Low income clinics | YWCA |

## Table 2–2. SAMPLE LIST OF CROSS-REFERENCES

**In addition to listing telephone numbers under the titles in Table 2–1, consider listing appropriate agencies and their phone numbers under the following headings. The trick to cross-referencing resources is to list each resource under as many headings as possible.**

| | |
|---|---|
| Abuse: alcohol | Labor relations |
|     child | Language |
|     drug | Learning disabilities |
|     elderly | Nurse specialists |
|     sexual | Pregnancy |
|     spouse | Premenstrual syndrome |
| Cancer | Schools |
| Children's services | Special disease entities that may have |
| Counselors, counseling |    their own services: cerebral palsy, |
| Day care: children |    muscular dystrophy, AIDS, diabetes |
|     elderly | Special ethnic or religious services: |
| Developmental disabilities |    Catholic Pregnancy Service, Jewish |
| Family planning |    Service League, Southeast Asian Job |
| Federal agencies |    Training Center. List under the appro- |
| Financial aid |    priate ethnic heading. |
| Handicapped: mentally | State agencies |
|     physically | Support groups |
| Housing | Toll free numbers |
| Job: problems | Work |
|    sources | |
|    training | |

consistent, however, and it is in nurses' interest to be familiar with them.

Compiling a list of physicians interested in obtaining referrals is the first step in activating a physician referral service. Make sure the physicians on your medical staff have an opportunity to write down their interests, requests, and concerns. Send each of them a questionnaire and have them return it. Figure 2–1 shows sample questions you might ask. If potential problems emerge when you are compiling the

## PHYSICIAN PREFERENCE QUESTIONNAIRE

Physician name _____

Address _____

Telephone:    Office _____Exchange _____

Specialty _____

Special interests of your practice _____
_____

Special limitations of your practice _____
_____

Associates _____

Types of payment you accept:              Welfare/DSHS          yes _____ no _____

                                          Medicare             yes _____ no _____

                                          Commercial           yes _____ no _____

                                          L and I              yes _____ no _____

                                          Self Pay             yes _____ no _____

Will you see occasional indigent patients? _____
_____

HMOs/PPOs in which you participate _____
_____

What is the usual waiting time for an appointment at your office? _____

I would like the following types of patients referred to my practice _____
_____

I would prefer the following types of patients NOT be referred to my practice _____
_____

If a patient of mine calls after office hours:

    Have them call my answering service _____

    Evaluate the need to call me _____

    Handle the call and send me a follow-up report ____

    Other _____

Special requests or comments _____
_____
_____

**Figure 2–1.**

information on the questionnaires, such as misunderstandings about the nature of the service, have nursing management address those problems at a medical staff meeting.

List the participating physicians, along with requests and preferences elicited by the questionnaires, by medical specialty. Post the list. Or use file cards and arrange them by specialty in a rotary file or file box. Determine what medical services are available for indigent persons and post that list along with the names of physicians on your staff who are willing to see people who have no financial resources.

Several questions may present themselves at this point. Do you triage common problems appropriate for specialty care (such as ear or abdominal pain) to family practitioners or to specialists? Are there enough physicians and low income clinics for the poor? Is the medical staff able to come to a consensus on questions like these? Issues that could divide the medical staff and present a problem to nurses as they interact with callers need to be addressed swiftly by nursing management.

Once the ground rules have been established and the physician referral service has been implemented, the goal is to provide the public with access to high quality medical care and to provide the medical staff with referrals distributed in an equitable manner. Regardless of decisions reached by the medical staff and management about the service, there are three "musts" for all nurses making physician referrals by phone. They are:

1. Callers must be assessed.
2. Referrals must be appropriate.
3. Physicians must be treated fairly.

The most urgent concern on the part of physicians is the possibility of nurses inadvertently referring their patients to a new physician. It is imperative that all symptomatic callers be asked whether or not they have primary physicians ("a doctor who usually sees you"). When callers have doctors, assess and triage their problems and refer them to their own doctors unless triage guidelines direct otherwise.

A caller who does not have a primary physician and for whom a physician referral is a reasonable solution can be referred according to the guidelines of your facility. Giving the caller three physicians' names and phone numbers puts responsibility for choosing a doctor on the caller. This helps avoid difficulty if the caller doesn't like a doctor and preserves the credibility of the nurse and the service. Some institutions prefer the control associated with giving only one physician's name or making appointments for callers.

Each physician should receive the same number of referrals or an explanation of why the number is not equal. A simple crosshatch counting method, together with the original questionnaire, can be used. Doctors who are willing to see indigent people get more referrals than those who are not, because there are more poor people in need of doctors than there are rich. Individual physicians may need to be reminded of this.

Nurses must have excellent, open, and ongoing communication

with participating physicians and their staffs. The mechanisms for accomplishing this vary from such simple, effective measures as calling and chatting with doctors and their staffs, followed by periodic written updates on the service, to elaborate and time-consuming tracking mechanisms. The best way of getting responses from doctors when you need to intervene on the behalf of callers or when you need to bend the rules is to talk with doctors on an ongoing basis. Talking to them regularly also helps you solve little misunderstandings before they turn into big misunderstandings.

## WHERE TO GET HELP

The ability to maintain open, friendly communication with professional peers is essential for nurses in community outreach services. Your capabilities are enhanced by the number of your contacts and the number of people who understand what you are doing and respect your skills. Other nurses with expertise in specialty areas can provide information and resources in their specialties. They can also serve as bridges to physicians. Pharmacists, social workers, librarians, veterinarians, and representatives of social service organizations can be helpful in solving complicated or unusual problems.

## REFERENCE MATERIAL

Reference material in the form of books, public relations and teaching material, pamphlets, professional journals, and articles and news clippings are essential to a community outreach service. This material provides reference information on callers' problems, keeps the nursing staff up to date on professional developments, and serves a valuable teaching and public relations function. But it can quickly grow completely out of control.

Reference books, which provide information about anatomy and physiology, disease processes, and drugs, are necessary to answer questions about subjects not covered by the triage protocols. Asymptomatic callers with questions such as "What is the incubation period of chickenpox?" or "What is a subdural hematoma? I'm doing a term paper" are frequent. Research your answers to be sure of accuracy and consistency and to safeguard your legal position.

It will quickly become apparent which references you use most frequently. Keep those books where you can grab them quickly and put the others in a less accessible spot. Table 2–3 lists titles telephone nurses have found particularly helpful.

Information about community services, such as pamphlets and flyers, and articles from newspapers, magazines, and journals arrive all the time. They contain essential information but are infrequently used. Post them, or put them in a "current events" folder. After everyone has

**Table 2–3. BIBLIOGRAPHY OF HEALTH CARE REFERENCES**

Anatomy and Physiology text.

Beneson, A. S., Editor. *Control of Communicable Diseases in Man.* Washington, D.C.: Official Report of American Public Health Dept. 1984.

Berkow, R., Editor. *The Merck Manual.* Rahway, N.J.: Merck & Co., Inc., 1982.

*Beth Israel Diet Manual.* Lexington, Mass: Callamore Press, D.C. Heath & Co., 1982.

Boston Women's Healthbook Cooperative. *Our Bodies, Ourselves.* New York: Simon and Schuster, 1976.

Dictionary (such as *Webster's Ninth New Collegiate Dictionary*).

Emergency Nursing text.

French, R. M. *Guide to Diagnostic Procedures.* New York: McGraw-Hill Book Co., 1981.

Goldfinger, S. E., Chairman. *The Harvard Medical School Health Letter.* P.O. Box 2438, Boulder, Colo. 80302.

Hospital and affiliated facilities brochures and catalogues.

Howry, L. B., et al. *Pediatric Medications.* Philadelphia: J. B. Lippincott Co., 1981.

Kiely, J. M., Medical Editor. *Mayo Clinic Health Letter.* Mayo Clinic, Rochester, Minn. 55905.

Local telephone books, including Yellow Pages.

Massachusetts Medical Society. *Morbidity and Mortality Weekly Report.* C.S.P.O. Box 9120, Waltham, Mass. 02254.

Medical dictionary.

Medical Society Roster.

Medical-Surgical Nursing text.

Obstetric Nursing text.

Pediatric Nursing text.

*Physicians' Desk Reference.* Oradell, N.J.: Medical Economics Co., Inc., 1988.

*Self Medication: A Guide to OTC Health Care Products.* Oradell, N.J.: Medical Economics Co., Inc.

Stewart, F., et al. *My Body, My Health.* New York: Bantam Books, 1981.

had a chance to review them, file them by subject. A file drawer or a couple of three-ring binders work well. Go through the files occasionally and eliminate what is outdated and what has not proved useful.

Flyers and pamphlets for mailing to callers accumulate as well. These come in handy if compiled for quick reference. Arrange them in a file drawer or in a partitioned box. Keep them separated by subject and, again, don't be afraid to throw out what you don't use.

# The Nurse as Marketer | 3

Because of the competitive nature of health care today, any service offered by health care providers is evaluated for its potential to generate income. Telephone assessment as a service is no exception. The nurse on the phone is a direct link to the public, and is in a position to establish a personal relationship with hundreds of people. The quality of the interaction between the nurse and the caller determines whether the caller thinks of the facility at other times of need, whether the caller is aware of the facility's services, and whether the caller feels positively about the facility. Obviously, the marketing potential through such a service is tremendous, and providers often recognize this.

The relationship between nursing and health care marketing has not been good over the long term. Marketers have had little understanding of the role of nursing and have often perceived nursing as "the big budget eater." It is, after all, the largest department, the marketers say, and if you can trim it by 1% you can save a lot more money than if you trim, say, community relations by 1%. This is true, but not a favorable starting point for understanding. Nurses, at the same time, have perceived marketers as barely reputable manipulators of the public trust—not an altogether accurate representation either.

But the times are changing. Nurses are beginning to realize that skilled, professional marketing may, in fact, keep health care providers solvent, and solvency certainly affects patient care. It also affects nursing jobs. Marketers seem to be realizing that nursing is filled with professionals who deserve to be supported, and without whom even the most sophisticated advertising will fail to maintain a facility's reputation.

"The best way to compete is to develop lower cost products and services while building bridges to the people who make health care decisions . . . ." Nurses have always built bridges, both to the public, by providing patient care and advocacy, and to physicians, by providing quality intervention for their patients. Only recently, with the vision accumulated from their expanding roles, have nurses begun to view

**19**

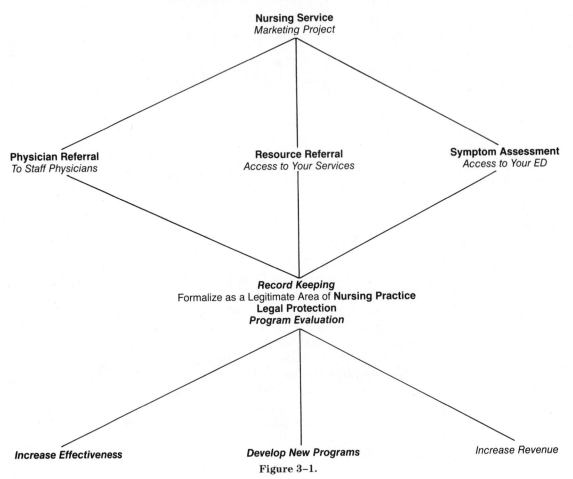

## COMMUNITY OUTREACH SERVICE

**Nursing Service**
*Marketing Project*

**Physician Referral**
*To Staff Physicians*

**Resource Referral**
*Access to Your Services*

**Symptom Assessment**
*Access to Your ED*

*Record Keeping*
Formalize as a Legitimate Area of **Nursing Practice**
**Legal Protection**
*Program Evaluation*

*Increase Effectiveness*

*Develop New Programs*

*Increase Revenue*

**Figure 3–1.**

these services as marketing. Community outreach nursing resembles more traditional marketing in several ways, as shown by Figure 3–1. The more professional and high quality the service, the more effective it is in generating community trust and loyalty. From a marketing perspective, community loyalty is the goal of these services.

There is concern among some nurses, when first participating in a nursing service with a marketing focus, that they are expected to manipulate callers in some way; to "bring them in" to the sponsoring facility. Manipulation is not necessary for this kind of marketing and, in fact, is counterproductive to a process dependent on mutual decision making. Although the health care system encourages a certain amount of inappropriate use, nevertheless teaching, support, triage, and facilitation of access encourage appropriate use while building bridges between the community and the health care system by meeting callers' needs. Figure 3–2 shows how this works.

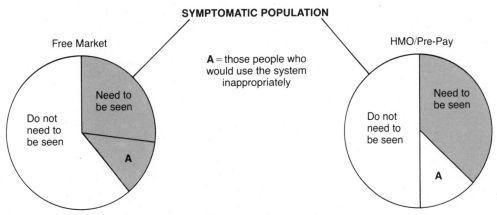

## COMMUNITY OUTREACH SERVICE: HOW IT WORKS.

Assumption: Through thorough assessment, the nurse increases
appropriate use of the health care system.

**SYMPTOMATIC POPULATION**

Free Market

HMO/Pre-Pay

**A** = those people who
would use the system
inappropriately

Need to
be seen

Do not
need to
be seen

**A**

Need to
be seen

Do not
need to
be seen

**A**

**A** is a significant number because both systems
encourage inappropriate use, but in opposite ways.

By increasing appropriate use, the outreach nurse:

**Increases visits** by those who
would stay home because of
negative financial incentives or
difficult access to a physician or
preferred facility.

**Decreases visits** by those who
would come in inappropriately
because of positive financial incentives or
easy access to a physician or
member facility.

TELEPHONE ASSESSMENT WORKS BECAUSE IT HAS AN IMPACT ON **A**
Figure 3–2.

There are, however, a few things you can do to make marketing your facility a little easier and more productive. Know what your institution offers and have information about its programs readily available. Consider keeping a separate file of your facility's programs; when you're looking for resources, check this file first. Mail information about your programs to callers who are interested. Ask callers, "*Have you been anywhere else before?*" "*Do you have a place in mind?*" "*Do you have a preference?*" If callers have no preference, encourage them to use your facility and its services. You support your institution by knowing what services it offers and by offering those services to callers who need them. Well-educated, satisfied clients who take responsibility for the health care decisions they make are the best possible advertising.

# Documentation

Documenting when you are on the telephone has inherent restraints. Your time is limited; there is always someone waiting. Writing space is limited; you have to be concise. You are writing down verbal information only, which requires special attention. In clinical settings, you often spend more time filling out the forms than you do with the patient; on the telephone, this is reversed. You spend as much as 95% of your time listening and talking compared with 5% writing. Skillful use of this small percentage of your time helps protect you legally.

There are no new rules for documentation in telephone assessment. They are the same ones you use in any clinical nursing area. The form you write on, the telephone log, is a medicolegal document just as progress notes are in a patient's record, so you use the same rules. We are not going to review those, but will list a few:

- Write in ink.
- Don't change entries unless you write "error."
- Write "late entry" and the date if you need to add something later.
- Use objective language.
- Be concrete.
- Be specific.
- Sign your log entry.

Although the basic rules for documentation are not new, when, where, and what you document are.

## WHEN TO DOCUMENT

Document right now, while you are talking to the caller.
Never wait until after you have taken the next call.

There will always be someone on hold, and you must become comfortable with this idea. You have a job to do for each caller, and it's not finished until you document the call. *Don't take the next call until you document.* There is a very good reason for this: you won't remember the call. That may sound impossible, but after talking to 10 mothers with sick children and 10 more callers with gastric distress, it all runs together.

## WHAT YOU DOCUMENT AND WHERE YOU DO IT

### Introducing the Telephone Log

Take a look at Figure 4–1. What you document is and should be straightforward and simple; it should also be brief. It will take practice to be good at it. As you will note, the space for you to write is small. The more clear and concise you are, the better the quality of your documentation will be and the sooner you can take the next call.

If you look at the boxes on the log, you will see categories for documenting the essential elements of the call: Caller ID, Reason for Call/ Assessment, and Response. But before looking at the specifics, there are some things that you document on *every* call from a symptomatic caller. These are the seven quality assurance criteria. They are measurable indicators, and they can help to protect you legally. With practice, you will remember them without difficulty because they make sense.

### What You Write on Every Call

#### The Quality Assurance Criteria

- Nurse ID (your initials)
- Caller ID
- Reference (name of protocol or other reference used)
- Alternate plan or follow-up
- Time of call
- Medication review checked (check "Yes" or "No" on every call)
- The presence or absence of chronic disease

These indicators are discussed in detail in the following sections.

If you look at the log again, we will talk about the specifics of what you document and where.

**Caller ID:** Write down what the caller tells you, or ask the caller to give you complete information including telephone number. Don't for-

# TELEPHONE LOG

DATE _____ PAGE _____

| T&I | Caller ID | Reason for Call/Assessment | Response |
|---|---|---|---|
| | AGE | | CR |
| | NAME | | |
| | PHONE | | MD R |
| | MD | | |
| | | CD | MED REV   Yes☐   No☐   PROTOCOL | ED |
| | AGE | | CR |
| | NAME | | |
| | PHONE | | MD R |
| | MD | | |
| | | CD | MED REV   Yes☐   No☐   PROTOCOL | ED |
| | AGE | | CR |
| | NAME | | |
| | PHONE | | MD R |
| | MD | | |
| | | CD | MED REV   Yes☐   No☐   PROTOCOL | ED |
| | AGE | | CR |
| | NAME | | |
| | PHONE | | MD R |
| | MD | | |
| | | CD | MED REV   Yes☐   No☐   PROTOCOL | ED |
| | AGE | | CR |
| | NAME | | |
| | PHONE | | MD R |
| | MD | | |
| | | CD | MED REV   Yes☐   No☐   PROTOCOL | ED |

**Figure 4–1.**

25

get to write down age and doctor; you will need this information in your assessment and response. If someone requests anonymity, put that down and ask for the caller's age and note whether the caller is male or female. If the caller is not the patient, note at least the first name of the caller, and then ask for the ID of the patient. At some point, determine the relationship of the caller to the patient. For instance, "Cheryl, mother of 3yo Nathan Smith" or "Mike, friend of 46yo Carol Frank."

**Reason for Call/Assessment:** This is where it is necessary to be clear and concise. You may have to do a lot of listening and clarifying before you write anything. You want to write the *real* reason for the call here, even if it's not the first reason the caller gives; this is where you write the *problem* as you begin the problem solving process (see The Process in Chapter 1).

Write the major concerns and symptoms from your assessment here, such as, "T 101°F., cough for 2 weeks, has no transp., is on welfare." If the caller is symptomatic, write down medications being taken. Write concerns or symptoms that affect the outcome of the call and that affect the decision you reach with the caller. When you are using a protocol, write the signs and symptoms the caller does have. Because you will name the protocol you use, you do not have to write down that they do not have the other symptoms listed.

At the bottom of the Reason for Call box are two small boxes labeled "Yes" and "No" with "Med Rev" in front. Med Rev stands for medication review. Refer to Table 1–3 for the components of the medication review.

Discuss each area in the medication review with the caller before you suggest the use of an over-the-counter medication; then check the "Yes" box. Although this is the only time you are required to do a medication review, there may be other times you feel the need to review these areas. In any case, for all calls, check "Yes" or "No," because this is one of the quality assurance criteria.

**Response:** This is where you write your responses to the identified reasons for the call or problem you have assessed. These may include:

- The mutual decision you have reached with the caller
- The solution agreed upon
- What you told the caller
- Information you gave the caller from a reference source
- Home care you suggested and reviewed with the caller
  If the caller is symptomatic, it *always includes:*
- An alternative solution

The quality assurance guidelines require that you work out an alternative solution with the caller in case the one agreed upon doesn't work. You might say, "If you can't get an appointment with your doctor, then you will _____"; "If you can't reach your friend, then you will try _____"; or "If the first solution doesn't work for any reason, then call me back." *Do this for your own legal protection* as well as to be sure that callers get what they need. If your communication skills have failed and you are uncertain the caller will follow through, write down, "seems hesitant." You can always ask the caller, "You sound a little hesitant; is there a problem with this solution?" Chapter 1 gives a complete discussion of the problem solving process. Once you are proficient with this process, you will rarely come to the end of a call with a caller who is still hesitant, and compliance will be very high.

There are additional boxes on the log:

- T&I. This is to write in the time and the initials of the nurse. Always write these.
- CR. Check this box if you refer the caller to a community resource.
- MD R. Check this box if you refer the caller to one of your physicians.
- ED. Check this box if you refer to your emergency department. You may want to count the number of callers you refer to these three areas. Checking the boxes makes this easier.
- CD. This stands for chronic disease. This is not a "yes" or "no" question. Explore the issue of chronic disease and document what the caller tells you.
- Protocol. Write in this space which protocol or other reference you used. Occasionally, circumstances dictate deviation from the protocols. When you deviate from a protocol, document the reason. What you write on the log must correspond with the protocol, or you must explain why it doesn't.

Last, document *all* calls, incoming and outgoing. If you plan to research something and call back, document that you are going to do that and then document the call back. Even document obscene calls and in-house calls. This is for your legal protection and it should be a standard program policy.

## QUALITY ASSURANCE

### The Audit

The assumption behind quality assurance is that measuring compliance to established standards improves service by providing information that can be beneficial in subsequent interactions. Measuring

**Table 4–1. QUALITY ASSURANCE GUIDELINES FOR HEALTH CARE ADVICE CALLS**

**The following should be noted for every call:**

Nurse's identification

Name, age, and phone number of caller or a notation that the caller requests anonymity; note age and sex

Time of call

Alternate or follow-up plan

Health care advice referenced by title and page of resource consulted or protocol named

Whether or not a medication assessment was done

Presence or absence of chronic disease

adherence to standards in a telephone encounter is unique because of the fleeting nature of the interaction. Once the call is over, the caller is gone. The only evidence of the interaction is the nurse's documentation. Quality assurance must, then, measure adherence to documentation procedures, because these procedures are the concrete, lasting expression of the nurse-caller interaction. Regular log audits are an easy way to measure adherence to documentation standards and to concurrently indicate the quality of assessment.

Table 4–1 lists suggested quality assurance guidelines, and Figure 4–2 shows a sample quality assurance audit. Regularly scheduled audits of 10 randomly selected calls per nurse give a clear indication of assessment patterns. Keep in mind that quality assurance guidelines apply only to health care advice calls (not to asymptomatic callers for physician referral, for instance).

## Follow-Through

Another issue unique to telephone assessment arises when looking at quality. Callers often have complex problems that can't be met immediately. Their questions need research. The issue, then, is to prevent those callers from "falling through the cracks" while solutions are investigated. A follow-through log achieves this. It places all unresolved problems in one place so you can find them easily. It allows you to research questions and return calls at a convenient time. You can avoid responses you might feel unsure of and still feel secure that callers' needs will be met.

Figure 4–3 shows a sample follow-through log. Keep in mind that this log is to inform staff about callers who need to be called back; it does not replace the telephone log. All calls are entered on the telephone log when they originally come in.

## QUALITY ASSURANCE AUDIT

Name: _____

Date: _____

| Call | Nurse ID | | Caller ID | | Time | | Alternate Plan or F/U | | Reference/ Protocol | | Medication Assessment | | Chronic Disease | | Comments |
|------|----------|---|-----------|---|------|---|----------------------|---|---------------------|---|----------------------|---|-----------------|---|----------|
| | Y | N | Y | N | Y | N | Y | N | Y | N | Y | N | Y | N | |
| 1 | | | | | | | | | | | | | | | |
| 2 | | | | | | | | | | | | | | | |
| 3 | | | | | | | | | | | | | | | |
| 4 | | | | | | | | | | | | | | | |
| 5 | | | | | | | | | | | | | | | |
| 6 | | | | | | | | | | | | | | | |
| 7 | | | | | | | | | | | | | | | |
| 8 | | | | | | | | | | | | | | | |
| 9 | | | | | | | | | | | | | | | |
| 10 | | | | | | | | | | | | | | | |
| % | | | | | | | | | | | | | | | |

Figure 4–2.

# FOLLOW - THROUGH LOG

| Caller Identification | Request | Done |
|---|---|---|
| Name: | | Date |
| Address: | | |
| Phone: | | Initials |
| Name: | | |
| Address: | | |
| Phone: | | |
| Name: | | |
| Address: | | |
| Phone: | | |
| Name: | | |
| Address: | | |
| Phone: | | |
| Name: | | |
| Address: | | |
| Phone: | | |
| Name: | | |
| Address: | | |
| Phone: | | |
| Name: | | |
| Address: | | |
| Phone: | | |
| Name: | | |
| Address: | | |
| Phone: | | |
| Name: | | |
| Address: | | |
| Phone: | | |
| Name: | | |
| Address: | | |
| Phone: | | |
| Name: | | |
| Address: | | |
| Phone: | | |
| Name: | | |
| Address: | | |
| Phone: | | |

**Figure 4–3.**

# Pitfalls 5

Pitfalls in telephone assessment are common errors nurses make without always being aware of them. They are not unique to this area of practice, but present a more acute risk because of the reliance on verbal communication. The absence of visual clues limits the information nurses have available for their assessment and presents a particular challenge to nurses unfamiliar with specialized communication skills. These mistakes are most commonly made by nurses inexperienced in telephone assessment and fall into two categories: communication and diagnosing.

## COMMUNICATION PITFALLS

### Not Listening

Unskilled communicators make several mistakes that can be broadly categorized as "not listening." They tend to "tune out" callers who are particularly long-winded or vague or whose grammar and speaking skills are limited. The temptation is to start thinking about a reply, rather than to continue listening. Such impatience is difficult to conceal. Learn to listen while callers tell their stories. Pay attention to content rather than form, and listen until the caller is finished. If you sense callers are going nowhere, begin directing and focusing rather than tuning them out.

Sometimes, nurses divide their attention by doing something while they listen. Doodling, scanning reading material, and going through files are all forms of not listening. They are frequently a sign of overload on the nurse's part. It's better to recognize them and deal with them as such, because callers can sense when you are not really listening.

### Overload: What to Do When You're Overwhelmed

If you are very busy for a long period of time, it's easy for your mind to become overloaded. You "go blank." It's very embarrassing if you are in the middle of a conversation, and it's a particular risk of fast paced telephone assessing. Learn to recognize the signs of impending overload and deal with them early. Put your other lines on hold and talk with one caller at a time, offer to take numbers and call back, put callers on hold to collect your thoughts, or take a break.

### Talking to the Wrong Person

Sometimes, the caller is not the person with the problem. Parents call for children, wives call for husbands, girlfriends and boyfriends call for each other. Adequate assessment of people over the age of about 10 is usually not possible through a third party. Ask to speak with the symptomatic person so that you get a true picture.

Occasionally, people call for others because there is some sort of disagreement occurring. "Mother has had a stomachache for 3 days. I think she should go to the emergency department, but she insists she isn't sick." "My sister's baby has a fever of 102°F. She says she will take the baby to the doctor in the morning, but I am really worried about the fever." When this occurs, talk to both people to sort out the facts, and negotiate a solution acceptable to both.

### Missing the Real Problem

If you miss the real issue, it may be because there is an emotion that the caller is not addressing directly. Either they are unaware they feel it, or perhaps they don't want to talk about it. More commonly, they don't know *how* to talk about it. For reasons of caller satisfaction and compliance, it is essential that emotional components be addressed. It is pointless, for example, to teach a mother how to treat her child's fever if one of her other children died of an illness that presented with a fever, and her real problem is terror. An accepting, nonjudgmental attitude combined with encouragement to explore the whole picture will usually elicit the uncomfortable emotion. With guidance, the caller can then begin to explore the emotional component of the problem.

### Taking It Personally

It is easy to get distracted by emotional words, especially if they are directed at you. Inexperienced nurses often respond inappropriately to emotion, particularly anger, and take it personally. Experienced listeners learn to distance themselves from the emotion, but not from the caller. They acknowledge callers' emotions. They also recognize their own emotions, but they retain their composure.

### Giving Up Too Soon

Some callers are particularly difficult to understand. They may have a language barrier, or include a lot of extraneous matter, or have a frame of reference completely different from the nurse's. These callers present a unique challenge because frequently their resources are limited and calling the nurse is their last resort. Try to listen carefully to these callers, sort through their stories, give feedback, and ask for confirmation of your impressions. The trick is to do this without becoming so frustrated that you give up or the caller hangs up. Some ethnic groups are particularly difficult to understand and are highly socialized to please. Sometimes these people hang up when they sense frustration. It helps to acknowledge your frustration and try a new approach. *"We aren't doing very well here, are we? I have lots of time, so can we try again? Tell me about _____ again."*

## DIAGNOSING

Diagnosing not only limits the information you obtain from callers, but also restricts your thinking and slows your growth as a communicator. The more open you are, the more nursing- and access-oriented, the more effective you are. Restrain your urge to diagnose—even when backed into a corner by callers. Develop new, more nursing-oriented ways of communicating. This can be difficult because callers have learned to expect a diagnosis. "Does it sound like I have the flu?" "Yes, it sounds like you have the flu" is an easier reply for a nurse whose experience with this concept is new, but ultimately, it seriously limits your thinking and your ability to communicate. Learn to explain what you're doing in nursing terms. *"I can't tell you whether or not you have the flu. But I can tell you about the seriousness of your symptoms, help you get the care you need, and tell you about some things you can do to help yourself feel better."*

### Leading the Caller

Leading the caller by asking "yes" or "no" questions too soon is a form of diagnosing. When you ask such questions, you take control of the conversation, which limits the amount of information elicited and the directions the conversation can take. It is a form of diagnosing because you have to have a diagnosis in mind to question in this way. Ask open-ended questions until you have a clear picture of the whole problem.

### Using a Protocol Too Soon

Using a protocol before you have the whole story and a clear picture of the problem is leading the caller with the protocol. It is a problem, again, because it restricts information gathering and limits your communication. It is easy, if you are inexperienced (particularly if you are afraid of missing things), to turn to the wrong protocol if you use your protocols too soon. The best assessors rely on communication and nursing skills, and use their protocols after their nursing assessment.

### Believing a Diagnosis, or
### Why There Is No Chickenpox Protocol in This Book

Chickenpox is a real problem. Most parents who call a nurse for advice about chickenpox are correct; their children do have chickenpox. Occasionally, however, a caller is wrong and the child has some other rash-producing disease. This book does not contain a chickenpox protocol because you should not accept a self-diagnosis—*even when you are sure the caller is correct;* even when the caller *is* correct. You must assess and triage the symptoms. Chickenpox is not the only example of self-diagnosing—but it is the best example. People frequently diagnose themselves, then call the nurse for advice.

The only time you can safely accept a diagnosis is when a caller has been seen by a physician and the physician made the diagnosis. Most of these callers, however, need information and assistance with problems rather than assessment of their symptoms. Callers with concerns about symptoms should usually be referred back to the doctor.

# Legal Considerations

6

## WHY WE WROTE THIS CHAPTER

There are very few lawsuits on record in which anyone, physician or nurse, has been involved because of telephone advice. So what is everyone worred about? Nurses, doctors, and legal advisors are all concerned. The reasons are clear:

- Emergency department nurses and office staff are called upon to give advice over the phone without guidelines, with minimal protocols, and often without documentation. On top of this, they have patients waiting, so telephone assessment becomes merely "answering the phone."
- People have a propensity to sue in our culture, and it's getting worse.
- There are no established standards of practice for telephone assessment.

The result is a potential for a lawsuit: there is inconsistency, there are no standards, and there is no quality assurance test. Does this make you feel vulnerable? That's why we wrote this chapter.

## HOW TO PROTECT YOURSELF

We suggest that you adopt documentation standards, use a quality assurance audit, and use the protocols in this book. Also, be aware of the pitfalls in assessment. If you follow these recommendations, you will decrease your legal vulnerability, but a quality assurance audit will not protect you if you can't make a good assessment.

### The Nurse-Caller Interaction

There are some things that do bear repeating. The nurse's interaction with the caller has crucial significance for legal protection. (We urge you to read Chapter 1 if you haven't.)

*The way to make a good assessment is to establish open communication and rapport with the caller.* The quality of your assessment depends on this. The well-informed caller who has chosen a solution to the problem through the interaction with the nurse is far less likely to sue than is the caller who is simply told what to do after a brief encounter. Mutual problem solving with trust and rapport leaves the caller feeling responsible for the decision and the outcome. There is no one to "blame."

### Compliance

A caller who has come to a decision about what to do with a problem is much more likely to comply with a plan than is the caller who is told the "best thing" to do. If you suggested a caller with children see a doctor, did you ask if the caller has a babysitter? Transportation? An alternative plan if needed? Greater compliance means callers are getting appropriate treatment, are happy with the assistance they receive over the phone, and are less likely to sue anybody.

### Diagnosing versus Access

Another legal pitfall which must be avoided is diagnosing. The use of protocols based on symptom triage rather than diagnosis frees the nurse to think about what's going on instead of thinking, "What's the caller got?" Symptom triage allows the nurse to concentrate on *access*. What do the callers need? Where should they go and how soon? How will they get there? Having a diagnosis doesn't help solve these problems. If you are asked directly, "What have I got?" always politely say, "I can't tell over the phone, but based on your symptoms, these are some of the ways you might get the care you need."

### Unsure Responses

Don't respond if you are unsure of yourself. Explain that you need to research the problem and call back. There may be times when something just doesn't feel right. In those cases, always recommend more conservative treatment and earlier medical care. If someone wants medical care, no matter how mild the symptoms, always assist them in finding it. Never tell someone who wants to come in not to do so.

## Callers to Handle with Caution

You should be very wary with certain types of calls. The following callers should be assisted with extreme caution and probably told they need to see or talk with a physician:

- People with chronic disease
- Pregnant women
- Parents of ill infants
- People who have had recent surgery
- People taking prescription medications
- Repeat callers

You can't acquire enough information over the phone to adequately assess these people. The parents of an ill infant should not be given advice (unless it's something as simple as diaper rash), nor should pregnant women who are ill.

A repeat caller is someone who calls you three times for the same problem. By the third call, you can assume you're missing something, and the caller should be assessed in person by medical personnel even if the problem is minor.

## Physician Consultants

Telephone nurses should have access to a physician consultant for medical questions and as an adviser to endorse the protocols. Ideally, the consultant would be certified in emergency and family practice.

Legal vulnerability in telephone assessment is not greater than in other practice areas. In any area of practice, the more skilled the practitioner, the greater the legal protection. In telephone assessment, verbal communication skills used within a problem solving framework are needed. As practitioners develop these skills, the legal concerns diminish. Along with the skills, standards are needed. When we adopt quality assurance standards, documentation guidelines, and protocols, legal protection is as assured as in other practice areas.

# Section 2

# The Protocols

# Using the Protocols

# 7

## INTRODUCTION

These protocols provide triage guidelines for callers with specific problems and associated symptoms. They are designed to be used quickly while talking on the phone. The protocols are arranged alphabetically by problem, with the problem heading at the top of the page as well as down the right margin. The entire protocol is visible as it falls open on opposing pages. (Pregnancy—Common Concerns is the only exception.) Each protocol contains a Home Care and Client Teaching section as well as relevant Nursing Diagnoses.

The triage format is based on access points into the health care system. This format arises from the concept of facilitating access as opposed to diagnosing and treating disease.

Most protocols are divided into sections based on four categories of assessment corresponding to access points and time frame (there are a few variations):
1. Immediate Intervention
2. Immediate Referral
3. Referral Within 16 Hours
4. Routine Appointment

Using symptom cues in each category, the nurse assesses which of these access points is appropriate for the caller's problem. The point is that the nurse is assessing symptoms to help callers decide where and when to access the treatment they need. Diagnosis, which is necessary for treatment, is never an issue using these protocols.

A couple of notes of caution are appropriate here. These protocols can be adapted for use in any facility that provides nursing assessment by telephone. The needs of each client population vary, and the protocols of each facility must meet the individual community's needs. Notice that each protocol has white space available for handwritten additions and deletions specific to individual client populations, facility policy, styles of practice, or nurse's comfort. Designate a person to assume responsibility for adapting protocols and devise a policy and procedure to support that person. Date and initial all additions and deletions.

In addition, the nurse practice act of the state in which the nurse is practicing imposes legal guidelines. Individuals using these protocols must be aware of the regulations that define their areas of practice and the extent to which these regulations control telephone assessment.

## WHAT THE PROTOCOLS DO

The protocols provide guidelines for assessing symptomatic callers and assisting them in managing their problems in a manner comfortable for both callers and nurses.

They regulate access through symptom triage.

They provide home care and teaching suggestions that adhere to nursing priorities and empower callers.

They provide assessment and triage consistency.

They provide advice consistency.

They focus on nursing priorities and the nursing process.

They provide for caller input into decision making processes.

They enable nurses to assess and assist symptomatic callers without chronic disease. A disease is chronic if it requires regular physician evaluation or regular medication or has been treated surgically. The one exception is diabetes. Diabetics have been included in these protocols because they are accustomed to assuming responsibility for their health management.

The protocols provide nursing diagnoses to focus decisions in nursing process terms and to facilitate thinking in new, more nursing oriented ways.

They include a section on how to assist parents of infants because the first months can be a difficult and trying time. However, nurses must exercise extreme caution when assessing infants.

This section includes an appendix on routine immunizations, because this information is often scattered and time consuming to locate. Appendix 1 provides current guidelines for immunization with the most common vaccines and anticipated reactions to them. It is a tool for caller education, not assessment. Symptoms are to be assessed by appropriate protocol.

## WHAT THE PROTOCOLS DO NOT DO

The protocols do not teach assessment skills. They are designed to be used by experienced nurses with proven communication skills and a thorough understanding of telephone assessment techniques.

They do not provide disease information. Disease information is available in other books. Nurses are expected to research disease entities to improve assessment skills.

They do not diagnose. For instance, there is no chickenpox or AIDS protocol. The protocols only assess rashes, fever, weight loss, swollen glands, and other signs and symptoms.

They do not provide medication information. The nonprescription medicines suggested in some home care sections are appropriate in the situations presented, but it is the responsibility of nurses to know the drugs they discuss.

The protocols do not provide a means of assessing the problems of callers with chronic disease. They do not take into account the special problems of people with liver failure, renal failure, congestive heart failure, or other such disorders. Nor do they take into account the problems generated by the drugs these people take: the steroids, the anticoagulants, the antihypertensives, or any of the myriad of other drugs they might take. *Attempts to assess callers with chronic disease using standardized protocols do not work.* Without medical records or physician consultation, assessment of these people poses special problems and risks.

# HOW TO USE THE PROTOCOLS

Using these protocols requires familiarity and practice. Get to know them. Read the protocol section thoroughly before you begin to use it. This section of this chapter describes how the protocols are used to assess and to determine effective interventions.

## Table of Contents

Become familiar with the headings of the protocols so you can use the table of contents to find protocols quickly. Become aware of the differences between protocols which may seem similar. Respiratory Distress and Wheezing, Extremity Pain and Joint Pain, and Depression and Suicide, Impending, for example, seem to be almost interchangeable protocols, but they are not.

## Index

Become familiar with the listings so that you can use the index to find problems and symptoms not listed as separate protocols. For example, infection is not listed separately, nor is bleeding. They are found under other problem headings. Puncture wounds, similarly, are mentioned within the Wounds, Minor protocol.

## The Protocols

Become familiar with the format so you can follow protocols easily. *Read the entire protocol each time you use it.* See the following pages for heading breakdowns and explanations, and follow a protocol as you read them.

After listening to the caller describe the problem, confirm that what the caller describes does, in fact, fall within the scope of the protocol by referring to the definition under the problem heading.

In each assessment section are signs and symptoms to be triaged as the heading specifies. Read through each of the sections while discussing with the caller the presence or absence of each of the signs and symptoms listed. You already know about most of them from your assessment. Use the protocols like insurance; they are to make sure you don't miss anything.

After assessing the caller with the entire protocol, discuss your recommendations using the appropriate triage category. Negotiate a solution comfortable for both yourself and the caller. Suggest home care as needed. Assess the caller's ability to understand and comply with instructions.

The caller may have symptoms from more than one section. Follow the most immediate intervention. If the caller has more than one problem, more than one protocol may need to be reviewed and the most immediate intervention followed.

# Problem Heading

### ASSESS FOR IMMEDIATE INTERVENTION

The signs and symptoms under this heading, when associated with the problem, indicate a crisis may be present. The community's Emergency Medical System should be activated. The caller should *not* be transported by private vehicle. Specifics of how the Emergency Medical System is to be activated will be determined by the caller. Assess the caller's ability and assist if necessary. Certain protocols indicate "See Home Care." If this is the case, refer to the Home Care and Client Teaching heading for interventions to be implemented until activation of the Emergency Medical System.

### ASSESS FOR IMMEDIATE REFERRAL

The signs and symptoms under this heading, when associated with the problem, indicate an emergency or an urgent care need may exist. The caller should be immediately referred to the most appropriate facility: emergency department, private physician, clinic, or other health care service. To determine which is most appropriate, consider established guidelines, caller preference, transportation, financial constraints, and the caller's ability to follow through. Certain protocols indicate "See Home Care." If this is the case, refer to the Home Care and Client Teaching heading for interventions to be implemented before transport to a medical facility.

### ASSESS FOR REFERRAL WITHIN 16 HOURS

The signs and symptoms under this heading, when associated with the problem, indicate that, although an urgent situation does not exist, medical attention is needed soon. For instance, some urinary tract signs indicate the caller does not need to be evaluated during the middle of the night or to leave work for evaluation, but can wait until a convenient time within 16 hours. Assist the caller in determining where to go, and assist with referral as needed.

### CONSIDER FOR ROUTINE APPOINTMENT

The signs and symptoms under this heading, when associated with the problem, indicate that medical evaluation is advisable, but the problem, unless it changes, is not harmful if not treated quickly. Assist the caller in determining where to go, and assist with referral as needed. It is assumed that 4 to 5 days is a reasonable wait for an appointment. If a caller must wait longer for an evaluation, other options may need to be explored.

# HOME CARE AND CLIENT TEACHING

This section is included for use after your assessment. The protocol, along with your assessment, will indicate when home care or teaching is appropriate. One or the other is appropriate in the following situations:

- Signs and symptoms may indicate home care is more appropriate than medical evaluation.
- Home care may be appropriate until the caller is evaluated by a practitioner.
- Home care may be appropriate for a period of time, after which, if symptoms persist, medical attention is indicated.
- Teaching is appropriate when it will prevent or modify the problem in the future.
- Teaching is appropriate when it will enable the caller to handle the problem without medical attention.
- Home care may be necessary while awaiting Emergency Medical System intervention or before transport to a medical facility. When this occurs, "See Home Care" is printed with the intervention heading. Refer to Unresponsiveness and Wounds, Major for examples.
- Home care may be appropriate to institute treatment for specific symptoms. When this occurs, the symptom will have a * or ** after it. This symbol directs you to the appropriate Home Care entry with a * or ** before it. Refer to Ear Pain and Hypothermia for examples.

# NURSING DIAGNOSES

This section is provided to refocus telephone assessment from a Medical Diagnosis Model to a Nursing Process Model. Nursing diagnosis assists in problem identification by naming caller problems amenable to nursing interventions. It defines interventions, home care, and teaching in nursing terms.

# Abdominal Pain

## ASSESS FOR IMMEDIATE REFERRAL

- severe or unrelenting pain
- traumatically induced pain
- difficulty walking upright
- guarding or clutching of abdomen
- infant with sudden onset of crying and flexed knees, lasting longer than 2 hours
- possible foreign body ingestion
- possible chemical ingestion
- bloody, tarry, or currant jelly stools
- right lower quadrant pain
- diaphoresis
- dyspnea
- extreme or unexplained anxiety
- missed menstrual period or documented first trimester of pregnancy
- rapid, irregular breathing
- diabetic spilling glucose and ketones
- ostomies

## ASSESS FOR REFERRAL WITHIN 16 HOURS

- fever
- sore throat or headache
- localized pain not in right lower quadrant and without guarding
- pregnancy beyond first trimester
- diarrhea or vomiting
- pain not relieved by Home Care
- pain with sexual intercourse

## CONSIDER FOR ROUTINE APPOINTMENT

- bulge in abdominal contour without pain
- mild, diffuse, intermittent discomfort
- menstrual cramps
- intermittent pain associated with school or work stress

*Discomfort or pain in the abdomen, including pelvis.*

► **HOME CARE AND CLIENT TEACHING**

*Instructions for Patient*

- maintain bed rest
- sip clear liquids
- consider aspirin or ibuprofen and hot water bottle for menstrual cramps
- apply pressure with hands on abdominal bulge when straining or coughing

► **NURSING DIAGNOSES**

- anxiety
- comfort, alteration in, pain
- coping, ineffective, individual
- fluid volume deficit, potential
- home maintenance management, impaired
- tissue perfusion, alteration in, cardiopulmonary
- tissue perfusion, alteration in, gastrointestinal

# Abused Child

## SUSPECT ABUSE AND REFER IMMEDIATELY—NOTIFY FACILITY OF IMPENDING ARRIVAL

- unusual or unexplained injury, especially in young child who was premature
- explanation of an injury sounds suspicious
- child less than 3 years old with suspected long bone fracture or loss of consciousness
- young child with alcohol or nontherapeutic drug ingestion
- trauma of external genitalia
- lower extremity burns or small round burns
- serious suspicion or fear of impending disastrous abuse

## ASSESS FOR IMMEDIATE REFERRAL TO A 24-HOUR CRISIS TELEPHONE HOT LINE

- overwhelmed caretaker with history of abuse or with fear of abusing— give numbers of support resources as well as crisis hot line
- caller who suspects abuse of child—give numbers of the local child abuse reporting agency

*Inflicted injuries, intentional drugging, sexual abuse, or neglect of a child. Consider appropriate protocols for specific problems.*

## HOME CARE AND CLIENT TEACHING

### Instructions for Nurse

- reassure overwhelmed caretakers that a nurse is always available at the number they have called (or at another number)

## NURSING DIAGNOSES

- coping, ineffective, family, disabling
- coping, ineffective, individual
- family dynamics, alteration in
- fear
- injury, potential for, trauma or sexual assault or both
- parenting, alteration in, actual or potential
- powerlessness
- social isolation
- violence, potential for

# Acne

## ASSESS FOR IMMEDIATE REFERRAL

- red, hot, tender facial skin

## CONSIDER FOR ROUTINE APPOINTMENT

- severe or extensive acne not responsive to 4 to 6 weeks of Home Care
- need for emotional support

*Skin eruptions and blemishes in the form of red bumps, whiteheads or blackheads, usually found on face, neck, chest, shoulders, and back.*

## HOME CARE AND CLIENT TEACHING

### *Instructions for Patient*

- clean t.i.d. with acne preparations or soap and water
- shampoo frequently
- eat a well-balanced diet
- remove makeup completely each day
- use hypoallergenic, water-based makeup
- avoid touching face
- apply benzoyl peroxide 5% or 10% once or twice a day after skin has been dry for 20 minutes
- decrease frequency of benzoyl peroxide application if excessive dryness occurs
- consider sun sensitivity when using both over-the-counter and prescription medications
- consider sensitivity to soap

## NURSING DIAGNOSES

- comfort, alteration in, pain
- coping, ineffective, individual
- home maintenance management, impaired
- injury, potential for, infection
- self-concept, disturbance in, body image
- skin integrity, impairment of, actual

# Allergic Reaction

## ASSESS FOR IMMEDIATE INTERVENTION–See Home Care

- all symptomatic persons with recent exposure to known antigen
- sudden onset of:
    facial swelling
    severe urticaria
    hives
    wheezing

## ASSESS FOR IMMEDIATE REFERRAL–See Home Care

- mild urticaria without known exposure to antigen or other symptoms
- any symptoms not listed elsewhere in protocol

## CONSIDER FOR ROUTINE APPOINTMENT

- chronic rhinitis and nasal congestion
- intermittent urticaria

*Histamine reaction to foods, inhalants, insect stings,*
*or drugs manifested by respiratory distress, tightness*
*in chest, wheezing, stridor, urticaria, angioedema,*
*rash, or nasal stuffiness. May be acute or chronic.*

## HOME CARE AND CLIENT TEACHING

### *Instructions for Caregiver*

- remove stingers from insect stings
- apply paste of water and meat tenderizer containing papain to insect stings for 20 minutes and cover with ice compress
- give oral antihistamine in appropriate dose if available and person has had drug before
- give injection from bee sting kit to person with insect sting if kit has been prescribed for person

## NURSING DIAGNOSES

- breathing pattern, ineffective
- fear
- gas exchange, impaired
- tissue perfusion, alteration in, cardiopulmonary

# Anorexia

### ASSESS FOR IMMEDIATE REFERRAL

- evidence of electrolyte imbalance

### ASSESS FOR REFERRAL WITHIN 16 HOURS

- extreme thinness and poor nutrition associated with anxiety and over-concern about weight
- anorexia associated with gorging and vomiting or laxative use

### CONSIDER FOR ROUTINE APPOINTMENT

- chronic anorexia unresponsive to Home Care
- fever, malaise, or other signs of acute illness

*Loss of appetite resulting in compromised nutrition.*

## HOME CARE AND CLIENT TEACHING

### *Instructions for Patient*

- Sip on clear liquids to relieve acute anorexia, especially if accompanied by nausea; Gatorade, tea, soda, and broth are well tolerated
- take small, frequent feedings of bland, high calorie foods such as milk shakes for anorexia of chronic illness

### *Instructions for Nurse*

- encourage mental health evaluation for anorexia with evidence of emotional component

## NURSING DIAGNOSES

- coping, ineffective, family, compromised
- coping, ineffective, individual
- fear
- fluid volume deficit, potential
- home maintenance management, impaired
- nutrition, alteration in, less than body requirements
- self-concept, disturbance in, body image
- self-concept, disturbance in, personal identity
- self-concept, disturbance in, self-esteem

# Athlete's Foot

 **ASSESS FOR IMMEDIATE REFERRAL**

- redness, swelling, or increased tenderness in skin surrounding the lesions

 **ASSESS FOR REFERRAL WITHIN 16 HOURS**

- signs of infection

 **CONSIDER FOR ROUTINE APPOINTMENT**

- Home Care not effective after 3 to 4 days

*A fungal infection causing itching and scaling of the skin on the feet, especially between the toes.*

## HOME CARE AND CLIENT TEACHING

### Instructions for Patient

- clean feet carefully with soap and water and thoroughly dry
- wear shoes that "breathe"
- wear cotton stockings and change often
- alternate pairs of shoes daily
- apply over-the-counter antifungal medication twice a day

## NURSING DIAGNOSES

- comfort, alteration in, pain
- home maintenance management, impaired
- skin integrity, impairment of, actual

# Back Pain

## ASSESS FOR IMMEDIATE INTERVENTION

- pain between shoulder blades
- sudden onset acute pain with dizziness, lightheadedness, or severe anxiety
- acute pain after injury—see Home Care*

## ASSESS FOR IMMEDIATE REFERRAL

- pain severe enough to prevent lying down or sleeping

## ASSESS FOR REFERRAL WITHIN 16 HOURS

- pain radiating to one or both legs
- discomfort with urination

## CONSIDER FOR ROUTINE APPOINTMENT

- mild to moderate pain not responsive to Home Care

*Pain located anywhere in the back other than the flank.*

## HOME CARE AND CLIENT TEACHING

### Instructions for Patient

* * *do not move* if back pain was caused by injury
* rest in bed
* lie on back in Gatch position
* lie on side with knees flexed and pillows under head and between knees
* use ice for 20 to 40 minutes every 2 hours for 48 hours; or ice and heat alternating for 20 minutes each every 2 hours for 48 hours
* consider using over-the-counter anti-inflammatory medication
* consider back strengthening exercises after acute episode has subsided

## NURSING DIAGNOSES

* comfort, alteration in, pain
* coping, ineffective, individual
* home maintenance management, impaired
* mobility, impaired physical
* self-care deficit, dressing and grooming

# Bad Breath

 **ASSESS FOR IMMEDIATE REFERRAL**

- fruity smell on breath
- evidence of diabetes
- evidence of alcoholism

 **ASSESS FOR REFERRAL WITHIN 16 HOURS**

- sore throat

 **CONSIDER ROUTINE DENTAL APPOINTMENT**

- bad breath unresolved by Home Care
- known gum disease

*Breath odor.*

## HOME CARE AND CLIENT TEACHING

### Instructions for Patient

- brush twice each day, brushing tongue lightly after teeth
- consider over-the-counter mouthwash or saline gargle
- floss teeth daily

## NURSING DIAGNOSES

- fluid volume deficit, potential
- self-care deficit, dental hygiene
- tissue perfusion, alteration in, cerebral

# Bites—Human & Animal

## ASSESS FOR IMMEDIATE REFERRAL

- large or dirty wound
- bites on hands, feet, joints, or face
- evidence of allergic reaction or systemic involvement
- multiple bites
- human bites
- any snake bite
- bites from known black widow or brown recluse spiders, or coral snakes—see Home Care*
- blister on site or purple discoloration of site
- severe pain
- muscle spasm or paresthesia

## ASSESS FOR REFERRAL WITHIN 16 HOURS

- signs of infection

## CONSIDER FOR ROUTINE APPOINTMENT

- person in need of tetanus update as indicated by Immunization Guidelines—see Appendix

*Trauma caused by a bite from human or animal. Tick bites—refer to Tick Bites protocol. Insect and other stings—refer to Stings—Insect & Marine protocol.*

## HOME CARE AND CLIENT TEACHING

### Instructions for Caregiver

* apply tourniquet proximal to bite
● observe all bites carefully for signs of infection

### Animal or Human Bites

● wash wound with soapy water for 10 to 15 minutes
● consult Public Health Department regarding rabies precautions for mammal bites
● confine animal

### Snake Bites

● clean wound with soapy water and antiseptic if available

### Spider Bites

● wash with soapy water, apply paste of water and meat tenderizer containing papain to site, and cover with ice compress for at least 20 minutes

## NURSING DIAGNOSES

● comfort, alteration in, decreased
● home maintenance management, impaired
● injury, potential for, infection
● skin integrity, impairment of, actual
● tissue perfusion, alteration in, cardiopulmonary
● tisue perfusion, alteration in, peripheral

# Breast Engorgement

## CONSIDER FOR ROUTINE APPOINTMENT

- monthly engorgement associated with menstrual cycle

*Hard, tender, swollen breasts.*

## HOME CARE AND CLIENT TEACHING

### Instructions for Patient

- try warm shower, massage, support bra, and manual expression of milk postpartum
- try manual expression of milk if milk is flowing too fast for infant to nurse comfortably
- use ice packs and support bra if pregnant
- apply binder and ice packs, and decrease fluids if nursing recently discontinued
- consider the possibility of pregnancy

### Instructions for Nurse

- reassure caretaker of newborn infant

## NURSING DIAGNOSES

- comfort, alteration in, breast tenderness
- comfort, alteration in, pain

# Breast Lumps

## ASSESS FOR IMMEDIATE REFERRAL

- hard, hot, painful area on breast, accompanied by fever

## ASSESS FOR REFERRAL WITHIN 16 HOURS

- pain unresponsive to Home Care
- discharge from nipple

## CONSIDER FOR ROUTINE APPOINTMENT

- any breast lump not associated with pain or fever

*Hard or soft mass in breast tissue, with or without tenderness.*

## HOME CARE AND CLIENT TEACHING

### Instructions for Patient

- massage lump for 15 minutes if nursing mother has hard, painful lump that is not associated with fever; continue nursing
- stop nursing if there is discharge from nipple; use breast pump for relief
- use hot packs for pain and redness not associated with fever
- consider aspirin or acetaminophen for discomfort if not nursing

### Instructions for Nurse

- encourage monthly breast self-examination

## NURSING DIAGNOSES

- anxiety
- comfort, alteration in, breast tenderness
- comfort, alteration in, pain
- fear
- home maintenance management, impaired

# Burns

## ASSESS FOR IMMEDIATE INTERVENTION

- extensive second- or third-degree burns

## ASSESS FOR IMMEDIATE REFERRAL—See Home Care*

- decreased level of consciousness
- extensive first-degree burns
- second-degree burns to face or genitalia
- second-degree burns larger than 1 inch in diameter on hands
- second-degree burns larger than 2 inches in diameter
- second-degree burns in person under 3 or over 60 years of age
- third-degree burns
- diabetics
- singed nasal hair or flash burns
- respiratory involvement
- coughing
- eye involvement
- increasing erythema, swelling, or tenderness
- purulent drainage
- decreased sensation

## ASSESS FOR REFERRAL WITHIN 16 HOURS

- failure to adequately care for burn

## CONSIDER FOR ROUTINE APPOINTMENT

- person in need of tetanus update as indicated in Immunization Guidelines—see Appendix

*Skin injury caused by heat, electricity, chemicals, or sun. The injury is classified by severity: first degree— erythema; second degree—erythema and blistered or broken skin; third degree—full thickness skin loss, absent sensation, charred or white skin.*

## HOME CARE AND CLIENT TEACHING

*Instructions for Patient*

* \* wrap extensive burns in clean, dry cloth for transport
* \* flush chemical burns with tap water
* treat small burns with cold compresses or cold water soaks for up to 2 hours; clean with soap and water and cover with dry dressing
* do not break blisters
* watch for signs of infection
* change dressing b.i.d.; clean well with soap and water during dressing changes
* consider aspirin for pain
* apply cold compresses and elevate for edema
* avoid ointment and anesthetic sprays
* avoid exposure to sun
* use sunscreens
* increase fluid intake

## NURSING DIAGNOSES

* comfort, alteration in, pain
* fear
* fluid volume deficit, potential
* home maintenance management, impaired
* injury, potential for, infection
* skin integrity, impairment of, actual
* tissue perfusion, alteration in, peripheral

# Chemical Dependence

 **ASSESS FOR IMMEDIATE REFERRAL**

- chronic alcoholic with evidence of withdrawal—refer to detoxification unit
- caller suspects ingestion and patient is extremely lethargic
- euphoria, flushing, vertigo, or itchy skin associated with use of opiates
- anxiety or panic reaction, hallucinations or exhaustion associated with use of amphetamines or hallucinogens
- dizziness, slurred speech, drowsiness, or ataxia associated with abuse of solvents
- agitation, paranoia, or exhaustion associated with cocaine use
- acute pain and fever or "cotton ball fever" immediately preceded by use of injected substances
- child who has ingested drugs—consider child abuse
- user who requests assistance, referral, or resources—refer immediately to Alcoholics Anonymous, alcohol and drug rehabilitation facility, or 24-hour alcohol and drug intervention telephone hot line

 **CONSIDER FOR ROUTINE APPOINTMENT WITH APPROPRIATE FACILITY**

- family or employment disruption
- school failure
- family member or friend seeking help
- evidence of drug seeking—refer to personal physician

*Prescription or recreational drug use resulting in abuse, addiction, or dependence. For evaluation of specific symptoms, refer to appropriate protocol.*

## HOME CARE AND CLIENT TEACHING

*Instructions for Nurse*

- encourage early alcohol and drug education for children, especially if an adult family member is an alcohol abuser or is chemically dependent
- encourage family members to attend a support group such as Al-Anon

## NURSING DIAGNOSES

- coping, ineffective, individual
- fluid volume deficit, potential
- home maintenance management, impaired
- injury, potential for, overdose
- skin integrity, impairment of, potential
- thought processes, alteration in
- violence, potential for

# Chest Pain

## ASSESS FOR IMMEDIATE INTERVENTION

- sensation of tightness, pressure, or squeezing
- substernal pain
- pain radiating to neck, jaw, back, or arm
- pain between shoulder blades
- nausea
- syncope or sense of impending syncope
- diaphoresis
- rapid or irregular pulse
- dyspnea in absence of other upper respiratory symptoms
- diagnosed angina pectoris not relieved by Home Care*
- severe or unexplained anxiety
- similar sensation to that experienced with previously diagnosed myo-cardial infarction

## ASSESS FOR IMMEDIATE REFERRAL

- acute pain caused by a fall or blow to the chest
- pain related to unusual muscular exertion involving the arms and aggravated by movement of arms
- upper respiratory symptoms

## ASSESS FOR REFERRAL WITHIN 16 HOURS

- diagnosed angina relieved by Home Care—notify physician

*Sensation of discomfort or pain in the thorax or ribs.*

## HOME CARE AND CLIENT TEACHING

### Instructions for Patient

* take prescribed nitroglycerin, one tablet sublingually every 5 minutes until pain is relieved, headache results, or three tablets have been taken
● rest

### Instructions for Nurse

● reassure and calm caller

## NURSING DIAGNOSES

● anxiety
● breathing pattern, ineffective
● cardiac output, alteration in, decreased
● fear
● gas exchange, impaired
● home maintenance management, impaired
● tissue perfusion, alteration in, cardiopulmonary

# Choking

## ASSESS FOR IMMEDIATE INTERVENTION

- inability to speak—see Home Care*
- inability to breathe—see Home Care*
- inspiratory stridor
- substernal or intercostal retractions
- gagging

## ASSESS FOR IMMEDIATE REFERRAL

- drooling
- coughing
- jaw locking
- inability to swallow

*Aspiration of a foreign body.*

▶ **HOME CARE AND CLIENT TEACHING**

*Instructions for Caregiver*

* institute Heimlich maneuver as directed by current American Heart Association guidelines
* if unsuccessful, begin resuscitative measures as directed by current American Heart Association guidelines
● avoid intervention unless airway is completely occluded

▶ **NURSING DIAGNOSES**

● airway clearance, ineffective
● anxiety
● fear
● gas exchange, impaired

**ASSESS FOR IMMEDIATE REFERRAL**

- projectile vomiting
- sudden-onset severe crying longer than 2 hours without apparent cause
- temperature over 101° F. or under 98° F.
- exhausted caretaker in danger of abusing
- flexed knees
- pulling on ears or rubbing head on bed
- caretaker who is excessively concerned

 **CONSIDER FOR ROUTINE APPOINTMENT**

- continuous crying for 3 or more hours every day at the same time of day

*Inconsolable, strident crying for extended periods of time.*

# HOME CARE AND CLIENT TEACHING

*Instructions for Caregiver*

- burp infant carefully
- use front pack carrier
- place infant in infant seat on top of running washer or dryer (do not leave infant alone)
- swaddle infant with a soft, stretchy blanket
- consider soy formula for bottle-fed infant
- experiment with diet changes if nursing
- comfort infant for 15 minutes, let cry for 15 minutes, and repeat
- place in windup swing
- let vacuum cleaner run; the sound will soothe the infant
- walk with infant face down with your hand under abdomen
- have infant lie with abdomen on warm water bottle covered by a soft cloth
- play a tape of mother's heart beat
- *spend at least a day* **away** *from the infant*
- take a shower during the screaming

# NURSING DIAGNOSES

- comfort, alteration in, pain
- coping, ineffective, individual
- home maintenance management, impaired
- injury, potential for, abuse

# Common Cold

## ASSESS FOR IMMEDIATE REFERRAL

- dyspnea
- inspiratory stridor
- lethargy and vomiting in child who appears to be recovering

## ASSESS FOR REFERRAL WITHIN 16 HOURS

- nasal discharge or sputum change from clear to purulent or green
- diabetic spilling glucose or ketones
- infant
- chest pain
- sensation of shortness of breath

## CONSIDER FOR ROUTINE APPOINTMENT

- persistent symptoms

*Mild upper respiratory symptoms, including rhinitis, headache, malaise, fever, and cough. Consider appropriate protocols for specific symptoms.*

## HOME CARE AND CLIENT TEACHING

### Instructions for Patient

- Increase intake of liquids
- use humidifier
- rest
- try nose drops made by mixing ½ teaspoon of salt, 1 teaspoon of baking soda, and 1 pint of water; use as needed
- consider acetaminophen for fever and discomfort
- consider oral decongestant or nasal spray such as oxymetazoline hydrochloride (Afrin) for temporary use by healthy adults
- place warm, moist towels on face
- use bulb syringe to clear nasal passages of infants and small children

### Instructions for Nurse

- emphasize good hygiene and hand washing to protect others
- remind diabetics to test frequently for glucose and ketones

## NURSING DIAGNOSES

- airway clearance, ineffective
- anxiety
- coping, ineffective, individual
- home maintenance management, impaired
- sleep pattern disturbance

# Constipation—Adult

 **ASSESS FOR IMMEDIATE REFERRAL**

- acute abdominal pain with vomiting or distention

 **CONSIDER FOR ROUTINE APPOINTMENT**

- unresponsive to Home Care
- recurrent constipation
- marked change in bowel habits with weight loss
- blood-streaked stools

*Hard, infrequent stools.*

## HOME CARE AND CLIENT TEACHING

### *Instructions for Patient*

- increase fluid intake
- eat high fiber diet, including bran, fresh fruit, fresh vegetables, prunes, and prune juice
- increase physical activity
- avoid laxative abuse
- consider bulk laxatives, such as those containing psyllium seed, for long-term management
- consider magnesium salts (milk of magnesia) for postoperative or postpartum constipation

## NURSING DIAGNOSES

- bowel elimination, alteration in, constipation
- comfort, alteration in, pain
- home maintenance management, impaired

# Constipation–Pediatric

## ASSESS FOR IMMEDIATE REFERRAL

- lower abdominal pain lasting longer than 2 hours

## ASSESS FOR REFERRAL WITHIN 16 HOURS

- anal pain or breaks in the perianal skin
- no bowel movement for 4 days in bottle-fed infant less than 1 month of age
- hard bowel movements with flecks of blood on the surface
- unresponsive to 7 days of Home Care

## CONSIDER FOR ROUTINE APPOINTMENT

- chronic intermittent constipation

*Painful passing of bowel movement or small, hard, infrequent stools.*

### ▶ HOME CARE AND CLIENT TEACHING

*Instructions for Caregiver*

- add 1 tablespoon of dark Karo syrup to each bottle
- mix prune juice 1:1 with 7-Up for older child
- increase child's intake of fruits, vegetables, bran, and liquids
- decrease child's intake of milk products, applesauce, bananas, and refined foods

### ▶ NURSING DIAGNOSES

- bowel elimination, alteration in, constipation
- comfort, alteration in, pain
- home maintenance management, impaired

# Cough

## ASSESS FOR IMMEDIATE REFERRAL

- cyanosis
- substernal or intercostal retractions
- diaphoresis and pallor
- lethargy or exhaustion
- infant with grunting cough and increasing lethargy
- sudden onset of inspiratory stridor during waking hours
- chest pain
- sensation of air hunger

## ASSESS FOR REFERRAL WITHIN 16 HOURS

- paroxysmal cough
- wheezing
- hemoptysis
- brown sputum
- fever and cough that is getting worse after 3 days of Home Care
- orthopnea
- green sputum after several days of coughing
- burning sensation in chest that is not responding to Home Care

## CONSIDER FOR ROUTINE APPOINTMENT

- acute cough not responding to Home Care
- chronic cough
- green sputum concurrent with onset of cough

*Involuntary muscle spasm to clear the airway.*

## HOME CARE AND CLIENT TEACHING

### Instructions for Patient

- increase liquid intake
- rest
- use humidifier at bedside
- try cough drops or lemon-and-honey mixture
- consider using expectorant, such as guaifenesin (Robitussin plain)

## NURSING DIAGNOSES

- airway clearance, ineffective
- breathing pattern, ineffective
- cardiac output, alteration in, decreased
- comfort, alteration in, pain
- coping, ineffective, individual
- fear
- fluid volume deficit, potential
- gas exchange, impaired
- home maintenance management, impaired
- sleep pattern disturbance
- tissue perfusion, alteration in, cardiopulmonary

# Croup

## ASSESS FOR IMMEDIATE INTERVENTION

- fear of impending respiratory arrest in child

## ASSESS FOR IMMEDIATE REFERRAL

- constant stridor
- dyspnea
- cyanosis
- inability to sleep
- drooling
- preference for sitting forward
- stiff neck
- suspected foreign body aspiration
- fever
- substernal or intercostal retractions
- inability to swallow
- acute episode unrelieved by Home Care

## ASSESS FOR REFERRAL WITHIN 16 HOURS

- child under 1 year of age
- intermittent stridor

*Upper airway inflammation usually occurring in young children and characterized by a harsh, high-pitched inspiratory sound and a barking expiratory sound or cough.*

## ▶ HOME CARE AND CLIENT TEACHING

### Instructions for Caregiver

- try sitting with child in steamy bathroom for 20 minutes to resolve acute distress
- try taking child into cool night air
- keep humidifier close to child at all times
- decrease milk intake
- offer clear fluids at 30-minute intervals

### Instructions for Nurse

- reassure caretaker

## ▶ NURSING DIAGNOSES

- airway clearance, ineffective
- breathing pattern, ineffective
- gas exchange, impaired
- home maintenance management, impaired
- tissue perfusion, alteration in, cardiopulmonary

# Dental Pain & Injury

## ASSESS FOR IMMEDIATE REFERRAL

- uncontrolled bleeding—see Home Care*
- avulsed tooth—see Home Care**
- jaw or facial swelling and fever over 100° F.
- pain not controlled by Home Care
- postsurgical fever over 101° F.
- injury to mouth with laceration larger than ½ inch, point tenderness on jaw, or decreased mobility

## CONSIDER FOR DENTAL REFERRAL WITHIN 16 HOURS

- acute pain controlled by Home Care
- broken tooth
- dental or gum disease
- loose teeth
- diabetic

## CONSIDER FOR ROUTINE APPOINTMENT

- intermittent pain

*Pain in the teeth or gums, postsurgical dental pain,
injury to teeth, mouth, or jaw.*

## HOME CARE AND CLIENT TEACHING

*Instructions for Patient*

\* apply pressure to stop bleeding
\*\* save intact avulsed tooth in saliva, or if not possible to use
  saliva, in milk, for 1 to 2 hours until dental care is available
- apply cold packs to injured area until seen by physician or
  dentist
- apply cold packs for postsurgical pain
- consider aspirin or acetaminophen
- apply warm packs to painful areas until seen by dentist if pain
  is associated with tooth decay or gum disease

## NURSING DIAGNOSES

- comfort, alteration in, pain
- home maintenance management, impaired
- injury, potential for, infection
- oral mucous membrane, alteration in

# Depression

## ASSESS FOR REFERRAL FOR IMMEDIATE CRISIS INTERVENTION

- severe depression, especially in adolescent, with precipitating event (divorce, death of spouse, loss of love)

## ASSESS FOR REFERRAL WITHIN 16 HOURS

- recent, unexplained onset, apparently coinciding with use of medication
- onset associated with increased use of drugs or alcohol—refer to appropriate chemical dependence program or counselor
- mild depression with history of psychiatric illness or hospitalization—refer to appropriate psychiatric resources
- inability to care for children

## REFER FOR MEDICAL EVALUATION OR COUNSELING

- menopausal woman
- cyclical depression, coinciding with last days of menstrual cycle
- recurrent, periodic depression
- interference with ability to carry out usual activities or work
- poor school attendance or school failure

*A feeling of hopelessness and helplessness associated with self-doubt, periodic crying spells, insomnia, anorexia, lack of energy, inability to make decisions, social isolation, school failure, aggressive behavior. Depression with suicidal ideation—refer to Suicide, Impending protocol.*

# HOME CARE AND CLIENT TEACHING

*Instructions for Nurse*

- encourage the following for mild depression not associated with drug or alcohol use:
  physical activity
  balanced diet
  social contacts
- give telephone number of crisis line or other support resource

# NURSING DIAGNOSES

- anxiety
- coping, ineffective, individual
- fear
- grieving, anticipatory
- grieving, dysfunctional
- injury, potential for, self-inflicted trauma
- powerlessness
- self-concept, disturbance in, personal identity
- self-concept, disturbance in, self-esteem
- sleep pattern disturbance
- social isolation
- thought processes, alteration in

# Diaper Rash

 **ASSESS FOR REFERRAL WITHIN 16 HOURS**

- open, oozing sores
- exposure to lice or scabies
- well-demarcated, erythematous areas with spreading pustules
- spreading rash
- rash unresponsive to Home Care

▶ **HOME CARE AND CLIENT TEACHING**

*Instructions for Caregiver*

- clean diaper area with water during each diaper change
- clean with mild soap only when necessary
- expose to air as much as possible
- use cotton diapers
- avoid plastic pants
- change diapers frequently
- apply ointment containing vitamins A and D and zinc oxide (Desitin) only while diapered
- try soaking diapers in diaper prewash
- wash diapers in hot water and use bleach every other washing
- double rinse diapers using vinegar in first rinse

▶ **NURSING DIAGNOSES**

- comfort, alteration in, decreased
- home maintenance management, impaired
- injury, potential for, infection
- skin integrity, impairment of, actual

# Diarrhea—Adult

## ASSESS FOR IMMEDIATE REFERRAL

- black, bloody, or tarry stools
- severe abdominal pain
- syncope
- lethargy and pallor
- menstruating woman using tampons
- decreased urine output
- light-headedness
- severe thirst
- absence of tears
- poor skin turgor
- profound fear or anxiety
- ileostomy

## ASSESS FOR REFERRAL WITHIN 16 HOURS

- cramping lasting 24 hours
- fever over 101° F. for 24 hours
- pregnant woman
- purulent or greasy stools
- diarrhea unresponsive to 48 hours of Home Care
- diabetic on clear liquids longer than 8 hours—consult with physician
- recent international traveler
- recent ingestion of water from lakes or streams

## CONSIDER FOR ROUTINE APPOINTMENT

- chronic diarrhea
- diarrhea alternating with constipation and unresponsive to 1 week of Home Care
- food- or drug-induced diarrhea unresponsive to Home Care

*Frequent loose or watery stools.*

## HOME CARE AND CLIENT TEACHING

*Instructions for Patient*

- maintain bed rest
- consider taking bismuth subsalicylate (Pepto Bismol) as label directs
- observe these diet restrictions:
    drink only frequent small amounts of clear liquids for 24 to 48 hours (such as diluted Gatorade)
    gradually add bland, soft foods
    add raw fruit and vegetables
    add grains and milk last
    add *Lactobacillus acidophilus* to diet if diarrhea is caused by antibiotics (yogurt is a common source of acidophilus)
- consider 1 teaspoon of psyllium (Metamucil) every 12 hours for diarrhea alternating with constipation and flatus
- decrease intake of dietetic foods containing sorbitol and mannitol
- consider antibiotics and antacids as a possible cause
- discontinue laxative use

*Instructions for Nurse*

- reassure
- instruct food handlers to remain off work

## NURSING DIAGNOSES

- bowel elimination, alteration in, diarrhea
- comfort, alteration in, pain
- fluid volume deficit, potential
- home maintenance management, impaired

# Diarrhea–Pediatric

## ASSESS FOR IMMEDIATE REFERRAL

- lethargy
- rapid or labored breathing
- poor skin turgor
- dry lips and mouth
- absence of tears
- no voiding for over 8 hours in child under 2 years of age
- no voiding for over 12 hours in child over 2 years of age
- more than two liquid stools in child under 3 months of age
- weight loss more than 5% of body weight
- one stool per hour for 6 or more hours
- bloody stools
- severe diarrhea accompanied by vomiting
- parent with serious concern
- diabetic child on clear liquids longer than 8 hours

## ASSESS FOR REFERRAL WITHIN 16 HOURS

- diarrhea unresponsive to 24 hours of Home Care
- temperature over 101° F.

## CONSIDER FOR ROUTINE APPOINTMENT

- chronic intermittent diarrhea
- diarrhea alternating with constipation

*Liquid stools or very soft stools with a water line.*

## HOME CARE AND CLIENT TEACHING

### *Instructions for Caregiver*

- continue to nurse breast-fed infant and give extra water
- discontinue milk or formula
- give clear liquids for 24 to 48 hours (consider giving an oral electrolyte maintenance solution such as Infalyte or Pedialyte to children under 1 year and diluted Gatorade to those over 1 year)
- increase to BRAT diet (bananas, rice, applesauce, and toast) and ½ strength soy formula for 24 to 48 hours
- consider yogurt with live *Lactobacillus acidophilus* culture for children on antibiotics
- discontinue child's intake of dietetic foods unless medically indicated
- maintain child at bed rest if possible
- keep child home from school and day-care

## NURSING DIAGNOSES

- bowel elimination, alteration in, diarrhea
- comfort, alteration in, pain
- fluid volume deficit, potential
- home maintenance management, impaired

# Dizziness

## ASSESS FOR IMMEDIATE REFERRAL

- third trimester of pregnancy
- severe headache
- ear pain
- sudden onset in person over 50 years of age
- history of head injury
- staggering gait
- vomiting
- history of acute or labile hypertension
- palpitations
- sense of impending loss of consciousness
- severe anxiety
- bleeding

## ASSESS FOR REFERRAL WITHIN 16 HOURS

- dizziness unresponsive to Home Care
- fever
- history of ulcers, hypertension, or anemia
- vertigo

## CONSIDER FOR ROUTINE APPOINTMENT

- recurrent dizziness
- intermittent brief episodes of vertigo
- dizziness precipitated by postural changes and not controlled by Home Care

*Sensation of unsteadiness or of surroundings spinning.*

## HOME CARE AND CLIENT TEACHING

*Instructions to Patient*

- restrict diet to clear liquids
- rest
- try keeping head flat
- discontinue alcohol, caffeine, decongestants, antihistamines, and pain medication
- maintain adequate hydration with extra liquids
- avoid sweets
- rise slowly from recumbent position
- if diagnosed with hyperventilation syndrome, try paper bag rebreathing
- consider the possibility of pregnancy

## NURSING DIAGNOSES

- activity intolerance
- anxiety
- cardiac output, alteration in, decreased
- fear
- fluid volume deficit, potential
- home maintenance management, impaired
- sensory perception alteration, kinesthetic

# Drowning, Near

## ASSESS FOR IMMEDIATE INTERVENTION–See Home Care

- respiratory arrest
- possible cervical spine injury
- cyanosis
- frothy sputum
- vomiting of swallowed water

## ASSESS FOR IMMEDIATE REFERRAL–See Home Care*

- coughing, crying, flailing, or otherwise responding to *short episode* of submersion that is not completely resolved in 5 minutes
- child under 3 years of age

*Nonfatal submersion of air passages. Immersion in*
*very cold water—refer to Hypothermia protocol.*

## HOME CARE AND CLIENT TEACHING

*Instructions to Caregiver*

* reassure and calm hysterical, crying, or coughing person and evaluate status in 5 minutes
* begin resuscitative measures as directed by American Heart Association guidelines
* remove victim from water while protecting neck by immobilization
* protect from aspiration of vomitus by turning victim on side

## NURSING DIAGNOSES

* airway clearance, ineffective
* breathing pattern, ineffective
* home maintenance management, impaired
* fear
* tissue perfusion, alteration in, cardiopulmonary
* tissue perfusion, alteration in, cerebral

# Ear Pain

### ASSESS FOR IMMEDIATE REFERRAL

- acute pain not relieved by Home Care*
- drainage from ear
- injury to head or ear
- fever or vomiting
- possible foreign body
- vertigo

### ASSESS FOR REFERRAL WITHIN 16 HOURS

- any ear pain not listed elsewhere in protocol
- hearing loss

### CONSIDER FOR ROUTINE APPOINTMENT

- sensation of fullness
- chronic intermittent discomfort
- ringing in ears

*Pain or other discomfort in or around ears, pulling on ears, or infant rolling head against bed.*

## HOME CARE AND CLIENT TEACHING

### Instructions for Patient

* consider aspirin or acetaminophen for pain
* consider warm compresses to relieve acute discomfort
* use humidifier to liquify secretions
* dry ears thoroughly with hair dryer after swimming in pools
* consider decongestant for well adults with sensation of fullness or mild discomfort; instruct in the need for regular use for 10 to 14 days

## NURSING DIAGNOSES

* comfort, alteration in, pain
* home maintenance management, impaired
* injury, potential for, infection
* sensory perception alteration, auditory

# Eczema

## ASSESS FOR IMMEDIATE REFERRAL

- redness, swelling, heat, and tenderness in tissue surrounding lesions

## ASSESS FOR REFERRAL WITHIN 16 HOURS

- itching that interferes with sleep
- yellow crusts
- purulent drainage
- fever

## CONSIDER FOR ROUTINE APPOINTMENT

- chronic rash not responding to treatment

*Acute and chronic inflammatory skin lesions occurring on face, neck, trunk, and skin folds characterized by erythematous patches of scaly, crusted, itchy skin. Caller must have been previously diagnosed.*

## HOME CARE AND CLIENT TEACHING

### Instructions for Patient

- avoid soap, chemicals, and alcohol based lotions
- avoid wearing wool
- bathe in tepid water
- apply lubricating cream after bathing such as Keri, Nivea, Lubriderm, or Sween Cream
- use hydrocortisone cream on itching areas, available over the counter in 0.5% solution
- use a humidifier during the winter

## NURSING DIAGNOSES

- home maintenance management, impaired
- injury, potential for, infection
- skin integrity, impairment of, actual

# Edema

## ASSESS FOR IMMEDIATE REFERRAL

- rapidly increasing edema in person with history of congestive heart failure or renal failure
- dyspnea or sensation of throat closing
- facial edema not associated with dental surgery
- generalized edema with rash
- edema of neck
- redness and warmth on face

## ASSESS FOR REFERRAL WITHIN 16 HOURS

- pregnant woman
- pitting edema
- periorbital edema without trauma or other signs and not responding to Home Care
- fever
- red, warm, tender edematous areas
- traumatic or surgical edema not responding to Home Care
- sudden-onset nocturia

## CONSIDER FOR ROUTINE APPOINTMENT

- dependent edema
- slowly increasing edema
- extremity edema not responding to Home Care

*Accumulation of fluid in tissues leading to swelling.*

> ## HOME CARE AND CLIENT TEACHING
>
> ### Instructions for Patient
>
> - rest
> - apply cold compresses to edema of traumatic or surgical origin
> - elevate edematous part on four pillows
> - decrease salt intake
> - discontinue alcohol intake
> - discontinue use of edematous part
> - apply warm compresses to warm, tender areas until evaluated by practitioner
> - apply cold compresses for mild periorbital edema
>
> ## NURSING DIAGNOSES
>
> - breathing pattern, ineffective
> - cardiac output, alteration in, decreased
> - fear
> - fluid volume excess, potential
> - gas exchange, impaired
> - mobility, impaired physical
> - skin integrity, impairment of, potential
> - tissue perfusion, alteration in, cardiopulmonary
> - tissue perfusion, alteration in, peripheral

# Electric Shock

## ASSESS FOR IMMEDIATE INTERVENTION

- respiratory arrest
- loss of consciousness
- extensive burns
- possible neck or back injury from fall
- seizures

## ASSESS FOR IMMEDIATE REFERRAL

- numbness and tingling
- burns
- palpitations
- pain
- headache
- fatigue
- any contact with current over 220 volts
- any small child, elderly adult, or pregnant woman

*Contact with electrical current.*

---

## ▶ HOME CARE AND CLIENT TEACHING

### *Instructions for Caregiver*

- treat brief asymptomatic contact with household current with cold compresses and rest

### *Instructions for Nurse*

- instruct caretaker of small child to cover exposed outlets, keep electrical cords in good repair, and avoid using extension cords

---

## ▶ NURSING DIAGNOSES

- breathing pattern, ineffective
- comfort, alteration in, pain
- injury, potential for, infection
- injury, potential for, trauma
- skin integrity, impairment of, actual
- tissue perfusion, alteration in, cardiopulmonary
- tissue perfusion, alteration in, peripheral

# Epigastric Distress

## ASSESS FOR IMMEDIATE INTERVENTION

- severe unrelenting or radiating pain
- hematemesis of more than very small amount of blood
- dyspnea
- diaphoresis
- severe anxiety

## ASSESS FOR IMMEDIATE REFERRAL

- acute pain
- hematemesis

## ASSESS FOR REFERRAL WITHIN 16 HOURS

- pain unresponsive to antacid therapy
- pain aggravated by eating

## CONSIDER FOR ROUTINE APPOINTMENT

- chronic intermittent distress
- distress not relieved by Home Care within 3 to 4 days

*Sensation of burning or pain in esophagus and stomach.*

## ▶ HOME CARE AND CLIENT TEACHING

### *Instructions for Patient*

- avoid caffeine, tobacco, alcohol, and spicy foods
- avoid eating prior to bedtime
- consider elevating head of bed
- try eating six small meals a day
- consider 1 to 2 teaspoons of a liquid antacid every 2 to 4 hours and at bedtime
- consider the possibility of pregnancy

## ▶ NURSING DIAGNOSES

- anxiety
- comfort, alteration in, pain
- fear
- home maintenance management, impaired
- tissue perfusion, alteration in, gastrointestinal

# Extremity Pain

## ASSESS FOR IMMEDIATE REFERRAL

- bleeding over site of extreme tenderness—see Home Care*
- traumatically induced deformity—see Home Care**
- severe pain
- extremity with cast or splint and with extreme pain or discoloration unrelieved by cold packs, pain medication, and elevation on four pillows
- sudden-onset numbness, cold, and pallor or cyanosis
- sudden-onset chest pain, dyspnea, or severe anxiety
- unilateral calf tenderness and warmth aggravated by flexing the foot
- child under 3 years of age

## ASSESS FOR REFERRAL WITHIN 16 HOURS

- severe swelling or discoloration
- joint pain with weight bearing
- signs of infection
- chronic pain, numbness, and pallor that is increasing in severity
- chronically impaired function

## CONSIDER FOR ROUTINE APPOINTMENT

- discomfort not responding to Home Care
- chronic cyanosis
- pain and paresthesia of arms or hands that wakes person at night and is aggravated by use of arms or hands
- pain aggravated by elevation and relieved by dependent position
- intermittent pain or discomfort
- diabetic
- leg cramps not responding to Home Care

*Discomfort or pain in upper or lower extremity.*

## HOME CARE AND CLIENT TEACHING

### Instructions for Patient

   \* cover bleeding sites
\*\* splint deformed injuries
- rest injured extremity; avoid bearing weight on injured leg
- elevate injured part on four pillows
- apply ice to injuries for 20 minutes every 2 hours for 36 hours
- change position frequently
- try moderate walking to relieve chronic discomfort and cramps
- elevate lower extremities to relieve edema and chronic discomfort
- avoid wearing tight clothing
- avoid applying heat to extremities
- avoid taping extremities unless instructed by practitioner
- avoid tobacco and alcohol
- try using cool, wet compresses to relieve chronic discomfort
- maintain good foot care:
    keep nails short
    cut nails straight across
    try Dr. Scholl's Foot Bath
- observe feet carefully for signs of problems
- massage skin with lanolin or Lubriderm
- wear heavy socks in cold weather
- try the following for leg cramps:
    increase dietary intake of calcium
    exercise
    take warm baths at bedtime
    avoid hyperextending feet
    try flexing feet
    massage legs and feet
    place a pillow under the covers at the foot of bed to keep
       weight of covers off feet

## NURSING DIAGNOSES

- comfort, alteration in, pain
- home maintenance management, impaired
- mobility, impaired physical
- skin integrity, impairment of, potential
- tissue perfusion, alteration in, peripheral

# Eye Injury or Discomfort

 **ASSESS FOR IMMEDIATE INTERVENTION—See Home Care***

- object impaled in eye

 **ASSESS FOR IMMEDIATE REFERRAL**

- suspicion of injury
- foreign body in eye
- visual disturbance
- chemical exposure—see Home Care**
- misshapen iris
- periorbital swelling or drooping
- pain with nausea and vomiting
- periorbital redness, swelling, and tenderness
- severe pain
- infant under 6 weeks of age with redness or discharge

 **ASSESS FOR REFERRAL WITHIN 16 HOURS**

- irritation or discharge with more than mild discomfort
- pain
- contact lens discomfort not resolved by 8 hours of Home Care
- severe photophobia
- nontraumatic, asymptomatic subconjunctival hemorrhage—refer for blood pressure check

 **CONSIDER FOR ROUTINE APPOINTMENT**

- localized inflammation of eyelid
- seasonal itching and discharge associated with rhinitis
- excessive lacrimation
- mild photophobia without other problems
- persistent discharge

*Trauma to or discomfort in one or both eyes.*

## HOME CARE AND CLIENT TEACHING

### Instructions for Patient

* avoid removing impaled objects
** flush eyes that have had contact with chemicals or toxic gas copiously before transport
* treat localized inflammation of eyelid with warm compresses every 2 hours
* consider antihistamines for seasonal irritation
* treat mild discomfort with cool compresses
* treat discharge with warm water, cleaning every 2 hours. Use clean cotton balls and maintain good handwashing.

### Instructions for Nurse

* suggest visual rest, including removal of contact lenses

## NURSING DIAGNOSES

* comfort, alteration in, pain
* sensory perception alteration, visual

# Facial Swelling

## ASSESS FOR IMMEDIATE INTERVENTION

- respiratory distress
- sensation of tightness in throat

## ASSESS FOR IMMEDIATE REFERRAL

- any significant facial swelling not associated with dental surgery
- ear pain
- dental pain
- traumatically induced periorbital swelling or drooping
- swelling that is red and warm to the touch

## ASSESS FOR REFERRAL WITHIN 16 HOURS

- third trimester of pregnancy
- mild puffiness associated with nasal discharge and tenderness over sinuses

## CONSIDER FOR ROUTINE APPOINTMENT

- mild puffiness with known allergies to grasses, trees, weeds, or dust

*Swelling on face.*

## HOME CARE AND CLIENT TEACHING

*Instructions for Patient*

- try cold packs on puffy eyes
- consider antihistamines to relieve exacerbation of allergic symptoms
- use cold compress for 20 minutes on forehead hematoma not associated with other signs of head injury

## NURSING DIAGNOSES

- breathing pattern, ineffective
- comfort, alteration in, pain
- home maintenance management, impaired
- injury, potential for, infection
- tissue perfusion, alteration in, peripheral

# Fever

## ASSESS FOR IMMEDIATE REFERRAL

- seizures
- stiff, painful neck
- profound lethargy or irritability
- infant with fever
- abdominal pain in right lower quadrant
- dysuria, frequency and urgency of urination, or flank pain
- facial swelling
- disorientation
- temperature of 103° F. not responding to Home Care
- temperature of 105° F.
- postsurgical temperature above 102° F.
- diabetic spilling glucose and ketones
- swollen, peeling hands and rash
- ear pain

## ASSESS FOR REFERRAL WITHIN 16 HOURS

- sore throat and swollen lymph nodes
- productive cough
- vomiting
- postsurgical temperature over 101° F.
- rash
- mild abdominal pain

## CONSIDER FOR ROUTINE APPOINTMENT

- intermittent fever
- fever lasting longer than 3 days

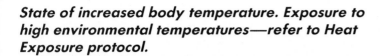

*State of increased body temperature. Exposure to high environmental temperatures—refer to Heat Exposure protocol.*

## ▶ HOME CARE AND CLIENT TEACHING

### *Instructions for Caregiver*

- encourage rest
- clothe lightly
- encourage increased intake of liquids
- treat children with temperature over 101° F. with acetaminophen every 3 to 4 hours as needed; adults may use aspirin or acetaminophen
- treat temperature of 103° F. with tub or sink bath in lukewarm or cool water for 15 to 20 minutes; sponge gently; do not towel dry

### *Instructions for Nurse*

- instruct diabetic to test for glucose and ketones q.i.d.
- instruct caregiver of small child in the use of rectal thermometer

## ▶ NURSING DIAGNOSES

- fluid volume deficit, potential
- home maintenance management, impaired
- tissue perfusion, alteration in, cerebral
- tissue perfusion, alteration in, peripheral
- tissue perfusion, alteration in, renal

# Flank Pain

 **ASSESS FOR IMMEDIATE REFERRAL**

- acute pain
- traumatically induced pain
- vomiting
- dyspnea
- fever over 101° F.

 **ASSESS FOR REFERRAL WITHIN 16 HOURS**

- low grade fever and malaise
- frequency and urgency of urination with dysuria or hematuria
- history of pyelonephritis
- history of renal calculi

 **CONSIDER FOR ROUTINE APPOINTMENT**

- continued discomfort not responding to Home Care

*Pain in the fleshy area of back between ribs and hip.*

## HOME CARE AND CLIENT TEACHING

### *Instructions for Patient*

- rest in bed
- try either ice or hot packs for 20 minutes every 2 hours; alternating hot and cold may decrease muscle spasm
- consider aspirin or acetaminophen for discomfort

## NURSING DIAGNOSES

- comfort, alteration in, pain
- injury, potential for, infection
- injury, potential for, trauma
- tissue perfusion, alteration in, renal

# Foreign Body in Orifice

### ASSESS FOR IMMEDIATE INTERVENTION

- sensation of occluded airway
- inspiratory stridor or croup

### ASSESS FOR IMMEDIATE REFERRAL

- pain
- bleeding
- foreign body in eye
- foreign body in ear, nose, throat, rectum, vagina, or urethra unable to be removed at home
- vomiting or chest or abdominal pain caused by swallowed foreign body
- sharp objects in any orifice or ingested sharp object
- ingested batteries

### ASSESS FOR REFERRAL WITHIN 16 HOURS

- radiopaque swallowed object

### CONSIDER FOR ROUTINE APPOINTMENT

- swallowed foreign body not found in stools

*Foreign body in any orifice or ingested foreign body. Aspirated or possibly aspirated foreign body—refer to Choking protocol.*

## HOME CARE AND CLIENT TEACHING

### *Instructions for Caregiver*

- consider *one* attempt at removal with fingers or tweezers if clearly visible
- kill live insects in ear by filling ear canal with isopropyl alcohol
- use blow dryer to clear disconcerting water in ears
- observe stools for passage of swallowed foreign body
- observe for vomiting, chest or abdominal pain, and bleeding if foreign body has been swallowed

## NURSING DIAGNOSES

- home maintenance management, impaired
- injury, potential for, trauma
- sexual dysfunction
- tissue perfusion, alteration in, gastrointestinal

# Hair Loss

## ASSESS FOR REFERRAL WITHIN 16 HOURS

- hair loss in conjunction with three of the following:
  lethargy
  cold intolerance
  menorrhagia
  scaly skin
  hoarseness
  periorbital edema

## CONSIDER FOR ROUTINE APPOINTMENT

- patches of hair loss
- hair loss not responding to Home Care
- chemotherapy-related hair loss—refer to local cancer society or support services

*Abnormal loss of hair.*

## HOME CARE AND CLIENT TEACHING

*Instructions for Patient*

- discontinue chemical treatments such as permanent waves and hair dye
- discontinue constricting hairstyles
- consider stress-relieving mechanisms

*Instructions for Nurse*

- reassure

## NURSING DIAGNOSES

- coping, ineffective, individual
- fear
- self-concept, disturbance in, body image

# Headache

## ASSESS FOR IMMEDIATE INTERVENTION

- loss of consciousness
- sense of impending loss of consciousness with sudden onset of "worst" headache the person has ever had

## ASSESS FOR IMMEDIATE REFERRAL

- traumatically induced headache
- stiff neck
- history of labile hypertension
- periorbital pain, vomiting, or visual disturbance without previous headaches of similar severity
- neurologic deficit
- fever and lethargy
- sudden onset of severe headache with cough, vomiting, or intercourse
- sudden onset of "worst" headache the person has ever had

## ASSESS FOR REFERRAL WITHIN 16 HOURS

- severe pain
- child with headache
- facial skin pain traveling along a nerve path
- vomiting
- sinus congestion with facial tenderness and darkened nasal discharge
- morning headache relieved by activity—refer for blood pressure check
- third trimester of pregnancy

## CONSIDER FOR ROUTINE APPOINTMENT

- tense facial, scalp, and neck muscles not responding to Home Care
- recurrent headache
- headache unrelieved by Home Care

## HOME CARE AND CLIENT TEACHING

*Instructions for Patient*

- rest eyes
- maintain quiet
- consider warm compresses if muscle tension is apparent
- consider cool compresses
- use humidifier
- consider caffeine withdrawal as a cause
- consider stress-relieving mechanisms
- sip small amounts of clear liquids frequently; try keeping iced liquids at bedside
- consider aspirin or acetaminophen for pain

*Instructions for Nurse*

- consider decongestants for well adults with upper respiratory symptoms
- reassure
- explore the possibility of drug-induced headache

## NURSING DIAGNOSES

- comfort, alteration in, pain
- coping, ineffective, individual
- home maintenance management, impaired
- tissue perfusion, alteration in, cerebral

# Head Injury

**ASSESS FOR IMMEDIATE INTERVENTION—See Home Care***

- neck pain
- loss of consciousness

**ASSESS FOR IMMEDIATE REFERRAL**

- scalp laceration
- bleeding nose
- black eyes
- black-and-blue mark behind ear
- drainage from ear
- difficulty rousing
- unequal pupils
- staggering gait
- confusion
- slurred speech
- increasing headache
- increasing drowsiness
- bizarre behavior
- visual disturbance
- memory deficit
- injured adult who vomits
- injured child who vomits more than twice or after 2 hours
- periorbital swelling or drooping

**CONSIDER FOR ROUTINE APPOINTMENT**

- intermittent headache
- ongoing concerns

*Fall or blow to the head possibly causing injury to the brain.*

## HOME CARE AND CLIENT TEACHING

### Instructions for Caregiver

* do not move if unconscious or if neck pain is present
* observe for 72 hours for all signs listed under Assess for Immediate Referral
* allow to rest and sleep
* wake after a "normal nap" and reevaluate
* restrict diet to clear liquids for 2 hours
* apply ice to hematoma
* notify family physician of injury

## NURSING DIAGNOSES

* memory deficit
* sensory perception alteration, visual
* skin integrity, impairment of, actual
* thought processes, alteration in
* tissue perfusion, alteration in, cerebral

# Hearing Loss

 **ASSESS FOR IMMEDIATE REFERRAL**

- traumatically induced hearing loss
- acute pain
- fever

 **ASSESS FOR REFERRAL WITHIN 16 HOURS**

- tinnitus
- sudden onset of decreased hearing

 **CONSIDER FOR ROUTINE APPOINTMENT**

- chronic hearing loss
- suspicion of hearing loss

*Decreased or absent hearing.*

## HOME CARE AND CLIENT TEACHING

### *Instructions for Nurse*

- encourage avoidance of loud noise, loud music
- encourage use of ear protectors when unable to avoid loud noise

## NURSING DIAGNOSES

- home maintenance management, impaired
- injury, potential for, infection
- injury, potential for, trauma
- sensory perception alteration, auditory

# Heat Exposure

## ASSESS FOR IMMEDIATE INTERVENTION

- stupor
- hot, flushed, dry skin
- rapid, shallow respirations
- temperature of 105° F. or above

## ASSESS FOR IMMEDIATE REFERRAL

- if more than two of these signs or symptoms are present *or* if any of these signs are present after 4 hours of Home Care
  weakness
  dizziness
  diaphoresis
  muscle cramps
  decreased urine output
  visual disturbances
  headache
  elevated temperature
  serious concern

*Exposure to high environmental temperatures.*

## ▶ HOME CARE AND CLIENT TEACHING

### *Instructions for Caregiver*

- undress
- move to a cool place
- sponge with cool water
- give sips of clear, cool liquids; a mixture of equal parts of Ga-torade and water is suggested
- elevate feet for edema of feet and ankles

## ▶ NURSING DIAGNOSES

- comfort, alteration in, pain
- fluid volume deficit, actual
- home maintenance management, impaired
- tissue perfusion, alteration in, cardiopulmonary
- tissue perfusion, alteration in, peripheral

# Hiccoughs

## ASSESS FOR IMMEDIATE REFERRAL

- respiratory distress
- fever
- pain
- acute anxiety

## ASSESS FOR REFERRAL WITHIN 16 HOURS

- persistent distress not responding to Home Care

## CONSIDER FOR ROUTINE APPOINTMENT

- recurrent hiccoughs

*Spasmodic contractions of the diaphragm.*

## HOME CARE AND CLIENT TEACHING

*Instructions for Patient*

- hold breath
- breathe into paper bag
- pinch nostrils closed and drink glass of water
- try 2 teaspoons of liquid antacid
- take a nap

## NURSING DIAGNOSES

- breathing pattern, ineffective
- cardiac output, alteration in, decreased
- comfort, alteration in, pain
- sleep pattern disturbance

# Hoarseness

 **ASSESS FOR IMMEDIATE REFERRAL**

- sensation of dyspnea or air hunger

 **ASSESS FOR REFERRAL WITHIN 16 HOURS**

- sore throat or cough accompanied by a fever

 **CONSIDER FOR ROUTINE APPOINTMENT**

- persistent hoarseness

*Deepening of voice accompanied by rasping.*

# HOME CARE AND CLIENT TEACHING

*Instructions for Patient*

- avoid speaking
- use humidifier
- increase fluid intake

# NURSING DIAGNOSES

- airway clearance, ineffective
- breathing pattern, ineffective
- comfort, alteration in, pain

# Hyperventilation

## ASSESS FOR IMMEDIATE REFERRAL

- injury
- pain
- substernal or intercostal retractions on inspiration
- increased thirst, urination, weight loss, or fatigue
- diabetic
- chest tightness, dyspnea, severe anxiety, or syncope without previously diagnosed hyperventilation syndrome
- acute anxiety

## ASSESS FOR REFERRAL WITHIN 16 HOURS

- previously diagnosed hyperventilation syndrome not responding to Home Care
- continued concern regardless of responsiveness to Home Care

*Rapid breathing, either shallow or deep.*

## HOME CARE AND CLIENT TEACHING

### Instructions for Patient

- rest
- breathe into paper bag for 10 minutes, stop for 5 minutes, and repeat procedure once
- use stress reduction mechanisms

### Instructions for Nurse

- reassure

## NURSING DIAGNOSES

- breathing pattern, ineffective
- comfort, alteration in, pain
- coping, ineffective, individual
- fear
- gas exchange, impaired
- home maintenance management, impaired

# Hypothermia

## ASSESS FOR IMMEDIATE INTERVENTION—See Home Care*

- temperature below 95° F.
- bradycardia
- slow respirations
- extreme lassitude, irrationality, or unconsciousness
- lack of shivering with documented prolonged or severe exposure

## ASSESS FOR IMMEDIATE REFERRAL—See Home Care**

- shivering and decreased mobility
- impaired thought processes and difficulty speaking
- white or blistered skin on fingers, toes, or exposed skin surfaces
- decreased sensation or acute pain in fingers, toes, or exposed skin surfaces
- alcohol or drug ingestion

*Lowered core body temperature due to exposure to environmental cold.*

## HOME CARE AND CLIENT TEACHING

### Instructions for Caregiver

* *do not move.* Remove wet clothing from person and cover with warm blankets. Remove your clothing and warm person with your body heat. Do all this with as little movement as possible.
** remove wet clothing and cover with warm blankets
● treat alert person with warm blankets and warm fluids administered orally

## NURSING DIAGNOSES

● cardiac output, alteration in, decreased
● comfort, alteration in, pain
● mobility, impaired physical
● sensory perception alteration, tactile
● skin integrity, impairment of, potential
● tissue perfusion, alteration in, cerebral
● tissue perfusion, alteration in, peripheral

# Incontinence

## ASSESS FOR IMMEDIATE REFERRAL

- trauma to rectum or urethra
- foreign body in orifice or ingested foreign body

## ASSESS FOR REFERRAL WITHIN 16 HOURS

- symptoms of urinary tract infection
- loss of stools through urethra

## CONSIDER FOR ROUTINE APPOINTMENT

- chronic incontinence, either fecal or urinary
- loss of urine on coughing, straining, sneezing, or lifting
- evidence of behavioral component in school-age child

*Loss of voluntary control of defecation; involuntary loss of urine during the day or night.*

## HOME CARE AND CLIENT TEACHING

### *Instructions for Patient*

- consider dietary measures such as eating prunes and fresh fruits
- eat meals and snacks at regular times
- try low residue diet for fecal incontinence
- perform sphincter contraction exercises daily
- consider biofeedback conditioning
- attempt to keep perineum clean, dry, and odor-free
- schedule regular toilet times
- reduce stress, anger, and anxiety levels

## NURSING DIAGNOSES

- bowel elimination, alteration in, incontinence
- home maintenance management, impaired
- injury, potential for, perineal skin irritation or infection
- self-image, deficit
- urinary elimination, alteration in, patterns

# Insomnia

## ASSESS FOR IMMEDIATE REFERRAL

- sudden-onset dyspnea during sleep

## ASSESS FOR REFERRAL WITHIN 16 HOURS

- inability to sleep without multiple pillows under head and shoulders
- emotionally related insomnia causing profound exhaustion

## CONSIDER FOR ROUTINE APPOINTMENT

- night terrors
- recurrent nightmares
- insomnia not relieved by Home Care
- diaphoresis during sleep

*Difficulty sleeping, or waking during the night.*
*Specific symptoms interfering with sleep—refer to*
*appropriate protocol.*

# HOME CARE AND CLIENT TEACHING

*Instructions for Patient*

- exercise daily
- take a warm bath at bedtime
- try hot water with lemon, hot milk, or Sleepytime tea at bedtime
- avoid eating large meals within 2 hours of bedtime
- consider stress reduction techniques
- avoid caffeine, decongestants, cocaine, and diet aids
- consider prescription medications as a possible contributor

# NURSING DIAGNOSES

- anxiety
- rest-activity pattern, ineffective
- sleep pattern disturbance

# Jaundice

## ASSESS FOR IMMEDIATE REFERRAL

- infant with lethargy, poor feeding, or vomiting
- intractable vomiting or signs of dehydration
- pregnant woman
- impaired consciousness

## ASSESS FOR REFERRAL WITHIN 16 HOURS

- fever and malaise
- nausea and anorexia
- swollen glands or lymph nodes
- clay colored stools
- concern about exposure to hepatitis
- infants

## CONSIDER FOR ROUTINE APPOINTMENT

- slowly increasing chronic jaundice previously diagnosed
- concern about exposure to hepatitis in person who is not jaundiced

*Yellow discoloration of skin or sclera caused by the body's inability to excrete accumulated bilirubin.*

## ▶ HOME CARE AND CLIENT TEACHING

*Instructions for Patient*

- rest
- maintain adequate nutrition
- discontinue alcohol consumption
- maintain personal hygiene
- maintain adequate household cleanliness

## ▶ NURSING DIAGNOSES

- fear
- fluid volume deficit, potential
- home maintenance management, impaired
- injury, potential for, infection

# Joint Pain

### ASSESS FOR IMMEDIATE REFERRAL

- severe, unrelenting pain
- traumatically induced pain
- sudden-onset joint immobility

### ASSESS FOR REFERRAL WITHIN 16 HOURS

- acute pain
- recent sexually transmitted disease
- history of gout
- rash
- fever
- involvement of multiple joints
- history of renal disease
- recent sore throat
- red, swollen, hot joint or joints

### CONSIDER FOR ROUTINE APPOINTMENT

- intermittent pain
- diagnosed arthritis not controlled by prescribed care
- temporomandibular joint pain with jaw movement

*Discomfort or pain in one or multiple joints.*

## ▶ HOME CARE AND CLIENT TEACHING

*Instructions for Patient*

- rest acutely tender joints
- consider aspirin for pain relief; if not tolerated, consider acetaminophen
- consider using heating pad set on low or hot water bottle on chronically inflamed joints; use if circulation is not impaired
- apply ice pack for 20 minutes every 2 hours to injured joint

## ▶ NURSING DIAGNOSES

- comfort, alteration in, pain
- home maintenance management, impaired
- mobility, impaired physical
- tissue perfusion, alteration in, musculoskeletal

# Labor

## ASSESS FOR IMMEDIATE REFERRAL

- sudden gush of fluid from the vagina
- contractions every 3 to 4 minutes lasting longer than 30 seconds
- vaginal bleeding
- severe abdominal or low back pain

## NOTIFY PHYSICIAN

- passage of mucous plug
- leaking fluid
- progressing labor with lengthening contractions of increasing frequency
- unclear concerns

*The physiologic process by which the infant is expelled during birth.*

## HOME CARE AND CLIENT TEACHING

*Instructions for Patient*

- change positions
- walk
- apply heat to lower back
- get a backrub

## NURSING DIAGNOSIS

- comfort, alteration in, pain

# Lice

## ASSESS FOR REFERRAL WITHIN 16 HOURS

- undiagnosed severe itching
- child less than 3 years of age with suspected infestation

## CONSIDER FOR ROUTINE APPOINTMENT

- infestation not responsive to Home Care
- repeated infestations

*Infestation of skin, scalp, or pubic area.*

## HOME CARE AND CLIENT TEACHING

### Instructions for Patient

- consider treating with over-the-counter preparation containing pyrethrins such as Rid or A-200 Pyrinate as directed; may be repeated once after 7 days
- wash combs, brushes, bed linen, and clothing with hot water
- vacuum carpets
- set aside hats and wigs for 2 weeks
- remove nits with fine-tooth comb; if difficult to remove, rub hair shafts with 70% isopropyl alcohol or mild vinegar solution
- examine household members
- notify sexual contacts

## NURSING DIAGNOSIS

- skin integrity, impairment of, actual

# Menstrual Irregularities

### ASSESS FOR IMMEDIATE REFERRAL

- severe abdominal pain
- pain in abdomen or pelvis after missed or late menstrual period
- fever, diarrhea, and rash during menstrual period if woman uses tampons

### ASSESS FOR REFERRAL WITHIN 16 HOURS

- missed menstrual period with extreme thinness and overconcern with weight, especially adolescent girls

### CONSIDER FOR ROUTINE APPOINTMENT

- missed menstrual period
- irregular menstrual periods
- cyclical fluid retention, breast tenderness, headache, or mood swings
- postmenopausal flow
- menstrual cramps unrelieved by Home Care

*Unusual occurrences associated with menstrual cycle.*
*Vaginal bleeding—refer to Vaginal Bleeding*
*protocol.*

## HOME CARE AND CLIENT TEACHING

*Instructions for Nurse*

- consider the possibility of pregnancy for missed or unusually light periods
- instruct woman to restrict fluids after 8:00 P.M., obtain first morning urine specimen for pregnancy tests, and refrigerate urine until brought in for testing

*Instructions for Patient*

- try the following for relief of menstrual cramps:
    rest or mild exercise; both seem to help
    aspirin or ibuprofen as directed
    hot water bottle or heating pad on abdomen
    increasing intake of dietary calcium

## NURSING DIAGNOSES

- anxiety
- comfort, alteration in, pain
- fluid volume deficit, potential
- home maintenance management, impaired

# Mouth, Lesions of

## ASSESS FOR IMMEDIATE REFERRAL

- facial swelling with tenderness, erythema, and heat

## ASSESS FOR REFERRAL WITHIN 16 HOURS

- fever over 101° F.
- enlarged, tender submaxillary nodes
- diabetic
- discomfort resulting in poor hydration

## CONSIDER FOR ROUTINE APPOINTMENT

- painless lesions
- lesions not responding to Home Care
- painful ulcers or vesicular lesions on erythematous base if person has never had them before
- known oral exposure to sexually transmitted disease—consider referral to sexually transmitted disease clinic
- white plaques with erythematous base on buccal mucosa, lips, gums, or tongue

*Single or grouped lesions on mouth or lips.*

## HOME CARE AND CLIENT TEACHING

### Instructions for Patient

- maintain adequate nutrition with liquids and soft, bland food
- maintain good oral hygiene with toothbrushing and rinsing with saline mouthwash three times a day
- try drinking with a straw
- try aluminum and magnesium hydroxide (Maalox) or other antacid mouth rinses as needed for comfort
- consider taking acetaminophen for discomfort
- try carbamide peroxide (Gly-Oxide or Cankaid) and Orabase on painful ulcerated lesions
- avoid contact with newborns and immunodeficient persons until lesions have been diagnosed

### Instructions for Nurse

- reassure caller if tender lesions are related to hot food or drink

## NURSING DIAGNOSES

- comfort, alteration in, pain
- fluid volume deficit, potential
- home maintenance management, impaired
- injury, potential for, infection
- oral mucous membrane, alteration in

# Neck Pain

### ASSESS FOR IMMEDIATE REFERRAL

- severe pain
- recent injury or auto accident
- pain or paresthesia in arms or hands
- high fever, lethargy, or vomiting
- extreme anxiety or sense of occluding airway

### ASSESS FOR REFERRAL WITHIN 16 HOURS

- swelling of submaxillary glands or lymph nodes
- fever
- respiratory symptoms

### CONSIDER FOR ROUTINE APPOINTMENT

- discomfort unresponsive to Home Care
- temporomandibular joint pain with jaw movement

*Discomfort or pain in cervical area.*

## HOME CARE AND CLIENT TEACHING

### *Instructions for Patient*

- rest
- try ice packs, hot water bottle, or heating pad, or alternating cold and heat for discomfort
- consider aspirin or acetaminophen for discomfort
- try supporting neck with a rolled towel collar

## NURSING DIAGNOSES

- breathing pattern, ineffective
- comfort, alteration in, pain
- injury, potential for, trauma
- mobility, impaired physical

# Nettle Stings

 **ASSESS FOR REFERRAL WITHIN 16 HOURS**

- spreading rash
- hives
- increased swelling, erythema, and pain

*Burning and itching often accompanied by a red, localized rash after contact with a nettle plant. The burning lasts from a few minutes to several hours, gradually decreasing.*

## HOME CARE AND CLIENT TEACHING

### *Instructions for Patient*

- apply ice or cold compresses
- consider antihistamine to relieve itching
- if plant is available, the juice from crushed *stem* of the plant is an antidote

## NURSING DIAGNOSES

- comfort, alteration in, pain or itching
- skin integrity, impairment of, actual

# Neurologic Deficit

## ASSESS FOR IMMEDIATE INTERVENTION

- sudden onset of impaired consciousness, or sensory or motor deficit accompanied by severe anxiety or respiratory compromise

## ASSESS FOR IMMEDIATE REFERRAL

- history of recent trauma
- sudden onset of:
    aphasia
    facial droop
    confusion
    visual disturbance
    dysphagia
    paralysis, paresthesia, or weakness of extremity or extremities
    increased deficit in previously impaired person
- pregnant woman
- ascending motor weakness, beginning in lower extremities
- recent ingestion of shellfish or home canned food

## ASSESS FOR REFERRAL WITHIN 16 HOURS—See Home Care

- intermittent numbness and tingling of extremities associated with diagnosed hyperventilation syndrome

## CONSIDER FOR ROUTINE APPOINTMENT

- increasing dysfunction in person with sensory or motor deficit or impaired thought processes

*Unexplained alteration of normal sensory or motor function.*

## HOME CARE AND CLIENT TEACHING

*Instructions for Nurse*

- reassure

*Instructions for Patient*

- breathe into paper bag for 10 minutes to relieve numbness and tingling associated with hyperventilation
- consider alcohol abuse as a contributing factor

## NURSING DIAGNOSES

- coping, ineffective, family
- coping, ineffective, individual
- home maintenance management, impaired
- injury, potential for, trauma
- memory deficit
- mobility, impaired physical
- sensory perceptual alteration, auditory
- sensory perceptual alteration, kinesthetic
- sensory perceptual alteration, visual
- skin integrity, impairment of, potential
- thought processes, alteration in
- tissue perfusion, alteration in, cerebral

# Newborn Infant– Common Concerns

## CRADLE CAP

Yellow, crusted lesions on scalp, possibly with facial rash.

***Consider for Routine Appointment***
- symptoms that persist or become worse

***Home Care***
- use mild baby shampoo daily

## CIRCUMCISION CARE

**Assess for Immediate Referral**
- tip of penis that is blue or black
- bleeding of more than a few drops
- swelling
- increasing redness
- purulent drainage
- tenderness

***Assess for Referral Within 16 Hours***
- concerned parent
- skin tag

***Home Care***
- rinse with warm water daily; if gauze is not off by the third or fourth day, soak with warm water and remove very gently

## JAUNDICE

For definition, see Jaundice protocol. About 50% of newborns experience physiologic jaundice appearing after 24 hours and normally disappearing in about 1 week. It is more likely to occur in preterm infants.

**Assess for Immediate Referral**
- lethargy
- poor feeding
- vomiting

***Assess for Referral Within 16 Hours***
- all others

*Exercise extreme caution when assessing infants.* **Any suspicion of illness** *indicates an evaluation is appropriate.*

## TEETHING

The eruption of baby teeth causing the gums to swell. Teething does not cause fever or diarrhea.

*Home Care*
- massage gums with ice
- provide smooth, hard object or teething ring for infant to chew on
- use cup temporarily if infant refuses nipple
- consider acetaminophen for pain

## UMBILICAL CORD PROBLEMS

Complications with the umbilical cord before it has healed.

### Assess for Immediate Referral

- tenderness
- red streak from umbilical area
- large amount of drainage
- spot of blood more than 1 inch in diameter
- fever

### Assess for Referral Within 16 Hours
- erythema
- swelling
- small amount of drainage

### Consider for Routine Appointment
- granuloma formation
- cord that fails to detach in 3 weeks

*Home Care*
- keep diaper turned down, and expose umbilicus to air
- clean once daily with cotton swab dipped in 70% alcohol
- do not use powders or ointments
- dry cord after bath

# Nosebleed

## ASSESS FOR IMMEDIATE REFERRAL

- severe bleeding uncontrolled by Home Care*
- headache
- impaired consciousness
- feeling of impending syncope
- dizziness
- trauma with deformity, broken skin, or orbital discoloration

## ASSESS FOR REFERRAL WITHIN 16 HOURS

- over 60 years of age
- intermittent bleeding poorly controlled by Home Care
- fever, sore throat, or respiratory signs
- known hypertensive

## CONSIDER FOR ROUTINE APPOINTMENT

- recurrent bleeding controlled by Home Care

*Bleeding from nares.*

### HOME CARE AND CLIENT TEACHING

*Instructions for Patient*

* blow both nares simultaneously to remove clots
* pinch both nares together and toward bony portion, holding firmly for 10 minutes
* apply ice to traumatic bleeds
• use humidifier to liquify secretions if respiratory signs are present
• apply petroleum jelly inside nares to keep mucosa lubricated

### NURSING DIAGNOSES

• comfort, alteration in, pain
• fluid volume deficit, potential
• home maintenance management, impaired
• injury, potential for, hemorrhage
• skin integrity, impairment of, potential

# Palpitations

## ASSESS FOR IMMEDIATE INTERVENTION

- chest pain
- dyspnea
- syncope or sense of impending syncope
- severe anxiety

## ASSESS FOR IMMEDIATE REFERRAL

- any palpitation occurring at time of call

## ASSESS FOR REFERRAL WITHIN 16 HOURS

- intermittent palpitations
- palpitations precipitated by a drug and persisting after discontinuing that drug

*The sensation of a rapid or irregular heartbeat.*

## HOME CARE AND CLIENT TEACHING

*Instructions for Patient*

- rest
- consider caffeine, decongestant, diet aid, or cocaine use as a contributing factor

## NURSING DIAGNOSES

- anxiety
- cardiac output, alteration in, decreased
- fear
- gas exchange, impaired
- tissue perfusion, alteration in, cardiopulmonary

# Penile Problems

## ASSESS FOR IMMEDIATE REFERRAL

- injury to penis
- more than a small spot of bleeding
- severe pain
- postsurgical temperature of 102° F.
- swelling and discoloration
- foreskin retracted and stuck
- persistent erection
- constriction by foreign body

## ASSESS FOR REFERRAL WITHIN 16 HOURS

- open sores, blisters, or warts
- purulent discharge
- spot of blood after intercourse—notify physician
- pain following ejaculation
- postsurgical temperature of 101° F.

## CONSIDER FOR ROUTINE APPOINTMENT

- itching without discharge
- abrasions
- impotence

*Discomfort, injury, or other problems with penis.*
*Burning on urination—refer to Urinary Discomfort*
*protocol.*

## HOME CARE AND CLIENT TEACHING

*Instructions for Patient*

- use good hygiene
- refrain from sexual intercourse until sores, itching, or discharge
  is treated
- use condom during intercourse if abrasions are present
- consider medication and alcohol use as possible contributors to
  impotence
- treat minor zipper injuries with soap-and-water cleaning and
  cold compress for 12 hours

*Instructions for Nurse*

- refer caller to sexually transmitted disease clinic when appropriate

## NURSING DIAGNOSES

- comfort, alteration in, pain
- injury, potential for, infection
- sexual dysfunction

# Perineal Trauma

**ASSESS FOR IMMEDIATE REFERRAL—See Home Care**

- acute pain
- laceration
- spot of blood more than 1 inch in diameter
- contusion with swelling or significant discomfort
- difficult or painful urination
- hematuria

*Injury to perineal area. Suspicion of sexual assault or child abuse—refer to appropriate protocol.*

## ▶ HOME CARE AND CLIENT TEACHING

### *Instructions for Patient*

- use direct pressure with cloth or sanitary pad to control bleeding
- avoid dislodging clots
- apply ice pack to injured area

## ▶ NURSING DIAGNOSES

- comfort, alteration in, pain
- injury, potential for, trauma
- skin integrity, impairment of, potential
- tissue perfusion, alteration in, peripheral

# Poison Ivy, Poison Oak, Poison Sumac

## ASSESS FOR IMMEDIATE REFERRAL

- exposure to burning plants
- respiratory involvement
- fever over 101° F.
- hematuria
- eye involvement
- headache and lethargy

## ASSESS FOR REFERRAL WITHIN 16 HOURS

- involvement of face or genitalia
- extensive open, oozing, painful rash
- increasing redness, swelling, and tenderness in skin surrounding rash
- enlarged lymph nodes
- fever

## CONSIDER FOR ROUTINE APPOINTMENT

- highly sensitive caller with high likelihood of exposure for consideration of prophylactic desensitization

*Known contact with antigen of poison ivy, poison oak, or poison sumac plant. Antigen is found in the resin present in all parts of the plant and in smoke produced from burning. Sensitization increases with exposure.*

## ▶ HOME CARE AND CLIENT TEACHING

*Instructions for Patient*

- wash exposed areas with soap and water immediately after exposure
- wash exposed clothing
- apply compresses of cool water or a topical astringent such as Burow's solution; keep them wet by covering with plastic wrap
- apply calamine lotion
- do not apply topical steroids without physician's evaluation
- wash open oozing areas with water; avoid soap
- consider antihistamines to relieve intense itching
- watch for signs of infection
- learn to recognize and avoid these plants
- do not burn plants; use weed killers if necessary
- consider family pet as a source of exposure

## ▶ NURSING DIAGNOSES

- comfort, alteration in, pain
- home maintenance management, impaired
- injury, potential for, infection
- skin integrity, impairment of, actual
- tissue perfusion, alteration in, peripheral

# Poisoning

## ASSESS FOR IMMEDIATE INTERVENTION

- respiratory depression
- lethargy or stupor
- seizure

## ASSESS FOR IMMEDIATE REFERRAL

- person operating engines or using chemical substances in closed spaces displaying confusion, nausea, flushed skin, or muscular twitching—see Home Care*

## ASSESS FOR IMMEDIATE REFERRAL TO POISON CONTROL CENTER

- any ingestion of toxic or possibly toxic substances

*Ingestion or inhalation of toxic substance or abuse of medication.*

## ▶ HOME CARE AND CLIENT TEACHING

*Instructions for Caregiver*

* move to well-ventilated open space
* give ipecac *if directed by Poison Control Center* before proceeding to medical facility:

    give 1 tablespoon with at least two glasses of water to persons over 1 year of age

    give 1 to 2 teaspoons with one to two glasses of water to children under 1 year of age

    repeat ipecac and water in 20 minutes if vomiting has not occurred

* lock up poisons and medications when small children are present
* consider having ipecac available at home

## ▶ NURSING DIAGNOSES

* breathing pattern, ineffective
* comfort, alteration in, pain
* gas exchange, impaired
* tissue perfusion, alteration in, cardiopulmonary

# Pregnancy—Common Concerns

 **ASSESS FOR IMMEDIATE REFERRAL**

- severe pain
- blurred vision
- gush of fluid from the vagina
- red, warm, painful calf
- heavy vaginal bleeding
- evidence of dehydration

 **ASSESS FOR REFERRAL WITHIN 16 HOURS**

- headache not responding to Home Care
- headache upon arising relieved by activity
- vaginal spotting, discharge, or itching
- no fetal movement for 24 hours
- blister or sore on vulva
- continuing facial puffiness
- nausea and vomiting not controlled by Home Care

 **CONSIDER FOR ROUTINE APPOINTMENT**

- any discomfort not relieved by Home Care

*Frequently encountered concerns associated with pregnancy. Evidence of labor—refer to Labor protocol.*

▶ ## HOME CARE AND CLIENT TEACHING

### Nausea

- eat small, frequent meals
- avoid sudden movement
- avoid greasy foods
- drink liquids between meals
- sip carbonated water or spearmint, raspberry, or peppermint tea

### Headache

- increase rest periods
- eat small, frequent meals
- apply hot water bottle or heating pad on low setting, or ice bag to forehead and back of neck

### Heartburn

- avoid greasy foods
- avoid coffee
- avoid cigarettes
- eat small, frequent meals
- rest with head slightly elevated
- sip liquids
- try walking
- try sitting cross-legged and raise and lower arms quickly, bringing the backs of your hands together over your head
- use low sodium antacids sparingly

### Stuffy Nose

- avoid inhaling irritants
- avoid cigarettes
- use a humidifier
- place warm, moist towels with hot water bottle on face
- increase liquid intake
- try saline nose drops: mix ½ teaspoon salt, 1 teaspoon baking soda, and 1 pint water in a clean, covered jar; use as needed

## HOME CARE AND CLIENT TEACHING *Continued*

### Constipation

- increase liquid intake
- increase exercise
- increase high fiber foods
- try prune juice and bulk-producing laxatives that contain psyllium, such as Metamucil or Effer-Syllium

### Backache

- wear supportive shoes with low heels
- exercise daily
- do prenatal exercises provided by practitioner
- apply hot water bottle or heating pad on low setting to lower back
- get a back rub

### Leg Cramps

- increase intake of dietary calcium
- exercise daily
- take warm baths at bedtime
- avoid pointing toes
- try flexing feet at ankles while sitting on floor
- massage cramped muscles

### Hemorrhoids and Varicose Veins

- wear loose clothing
- exercise daily
- avoid knee-high stockings
- wear support pantyhose
- avoid standing for extended periods of time
- lie down with legs elevated for 20 minutes four times a day
- try refrigerated witch hazel pads, such as Tucks, on hemorrhoids

### Ankle and Hand Edema

- rest with legs or hands elevated
- avoid tight clothing and knee-high stockings

### Difficulty Sleeping

- exercise daily
- take warm bath at bedtime
- drink warm milk or hot water with lemon at bedtime
- avoid eating large meals within 2 hours of bedtime
- avoid caffeine
- use pillows to prop knees, abdomen, head, and back into a comfortable position
- get a back rub

### Breast Tenderness

- wear a support bra with wide, nonstretch straps 24 hours a day
- use cool compresses or ice packs to provide temporary relief
- clean gently with minimal soap and rinse well
- avoid ointments and creams if they contribute to irritation

## ASSESS FOR IMMEDIATE INTERVENTION

- respiratory distress
- tightness in throat
- facial swelling

## ASSESS FOR IMMEDIATE REFERRAL

- urticaria
- fever over 102° F.
- headache
- sore throat
- stiff neck
- menstruating woman using tampons who has diarrhea
- lethargy or decreasing level of consciousness
- eye involvement
- hematuria
- fever and swollen, peeling hands

## ASSESS FOR REFERRAL WITHIN 16 HOURS

- open, oozing rash
- lesions surrounded by red, warm, tender skin
- pain
- involvement of mucous membranes or genitalia
- low grade fever
- cough
- pregnant woman with diffuse rash on trunk
- blisters, sores, or peeling skin on hands and feet and in mouth
- exposure to contagious disease or recent immunization—*consult with physician*

## CONSIDER FOR ROUTINE APPOINTMENT

- possible contact dermatitis not responding to Home Care
- diffuse, itchy rash after exposure to scabies or lice
- round, discrete, enlarging, and spreading lesions
- any rash not responding to Home Care
- red, itchy, peeling skin between the toes not responding to Athlete's Foot protocol
- known exposure to impetigo

*Diffuse skin changes.*

# HOME CARE AND CLIENT TEACHING

*Instructions for Patient*

- apply cold compress every 2 hours
- take baking soda baths (½ cup per tub) as desired
- apply calamine lotion to relieve itching
- use acetaminophen for discomfort
- consider antihistamines to relieve itching that causes sleeplessness
- treat dry, flaky, itching skin with mild lotion or cream such as Nivea, Lubriderm, or Sween Cream
- consider possibility of contact dermatitis related to exposure to soap, insecticides, skin creams, clothing, plants, or chemicals
- do not apply topical steroids without physician's evaluation
- wash hands after contact with involved skin
- avoid scratching
- avoid exposure to sun

# NURSING DIAGNOSES

- breathing pattern, ineffective
- comfort, alteration in, pain
- coping, ineffective, individual
- home maintenance management, impaired
- injury, potential for, infection
- skin integrity, impairment of, actual
- sleep pattern disturbance
- tissue perfusion, alteration in, peripheral

# Rectal Discomfort, Bleeding

 **ASSESS FOR IMMEDIATE REFERRAL**

- severe, unrelenting pain
- grossly bloody stools

 **ASSESS FOR REFERRAL WITHIN 16 HOURS**

- bleeding with bowel movement
- red color in toilet with bowel movement
- purulent drainage
- pain with bowel movement, unrelieved by Home Care
- pinworms observed on diapering of infant or examination by responsible person; notify physician

 **CONSIDER FOR ROUTINE APPOINTMENT**

- chronic discomfort
- acute intermittent discomfort relieved by Home Care
- traces of blood on toilet paper
- perianal pain and itching at night
- perianal excoriation

*Discomfort, pain, or itching of anus.*

---

▶ ## HOME CARE AND CLIENT TEACHING

*Instructions for Patient*

- increase exercise
- avoid prolonged sitting, standing, lifting, and straining
- reduce external hemorrhoids manually to relieve discomfort
- increase water intake
- drink coffee or warm water on arising to initiate a bowel movement
- increase intake of fresh fruits, vegetables, and bran
- consider bulk laxative or stool softener to keep stools soft and decrease discomfort
- try sitting in warm bath for 20 minutes every 3 to 4 hours and after each bowel movement to relieve discomfort
- use Tucks pads as directed twice daily and after each bowel movement
- consider over-the-counter hemorrhoid creams or suppositories such as Anusol

*Instructions for Nurse*

- stress personal hygiene in family with pinworm infestation:
    careful handwashing before eating and after toilet
    wear fitted underpants under pajamas at bedtime
    wash anus well and change clothing on arising
    wash bed linen, underclothing, and pajamas on day of treatment

---

▶ ## NURSING DIAGNOSES

- comfort, alteration in, pain
- home maintenance management, impaired
- skin integrity, impairment of, potential

# Respiratory Distress

## ASSESS FOR IMMEDIATE INTERVENTION–See Home Care

- respiratory arrest
- fear of impending respiratory arrest
- chest pain
- recent injury
- cyanosis
- acute anxiety
- allergen exposure
- suspected foreign body aspiration
- suspected overdose or toxic ingestion

## ASSESS FOR IMMEDIATE REFERRAL–See Home Care

- substernal or intercostal retractions on inspiration
- inspiratory stridor
- wheezing
- exhaustion
- sudden-onset dyspnea during sleep

*Respiratory depression or sensation of shortness of breath or air hunger.*

# HOME CARE AND CLIENT TEACHING

*Instructions for Caregiver*

- *be prepared to institute cardiopulmonary resuscitation* as directed by American Heart Association guidelines
- reassure
- avoid moving injured person
- help person into comfortable position if uninjured

*Instructions for Nurse*

- reassure caregiver and instruct to observe carefully

# NURSING DIAGNOSES

- airway clearance, ineffective
- anxiety
- breathing pattern, ineffective
- cardiac output, alteration in, decreased
- comfort, alteration in, pain
- fear
- gas exchange, impaired
- tissue perfusion, alteration in, cardiopulmonary

# Rhinitis

## ASSESS FOR IMMEDIATE REFERRAL

- rhinitis precipitated by head or facial trauma

## ASSESS FOR REFERRAL WITHIN 16 HOURS

- brown or green nasal discharge
- acute head pain

## CONSIDER FOR ROUTINE APPOINTMENT

- chronic nasal discharge
- acute nasal discharge not responding to Home Care

## ► HOME CARE AND CLIENT TEACHING

### *Instructions for Patient*

- increase intake of liquids
- use humidifier
- try warm or cool compresses to face; either may provide relief
- consider oral decongestant or nasal spray such as oxymetazoline hydrochloride (Afrin) for temporary use by well adults
- try nose drops made by mixing ½ teaspoon salt, 1 teaspoon baking soda, and 1 pint water for use as needed

### *Instructions for Caregiver*

- use bulb syringe to clear nasal passages of infants and small children

## ► NURSING DIAGNOSES

- comfort, alteration in, pain
- injury, potential for, infection

# Scrotal Pain or Swelling

### ASSESS FOR IMMEDIATE REFERRAL

- pain or swelling precipitated by trauma
- severe pain
- discoloration
- vomiting
- postsurgical fever of 102° F.

### ASSESS FOR REFERRAL WITHIN 16 HOURS

- lump or swelling not previously diagnosed
- postsurgical fever of 101° F.

### CONSIDER FOR ROUTINE APPOINTMENT

- intermittent, recurrent scrotal swelling with little or no pain

*Pain or swelling in the scrotum.*

## HOME CARE AND CLIENT TEACHING

### *Instructions for Patient*

- apply ice and elevate scrotum on towels for postsurgical problems
- apply ice for traumatic pain or swelling until medical evaluation can be obtained
- for periodic swelling, elevate scrotum on towels while recumbent until medical evaluation can be obtained

## NURSING DIAGNOSES

- anxiety
- comfort, alteration in, pain
- home maintenance management, impaired
- tissue perfusion, alteration in, peripheral

# Seizure

## ASSESS FOR IMMEDIATE INTERVENTION–See Home Care*

- diabetic
- suspected drug overdose
- seizure lasting over 1 minute
- evidence of compromised airway

## ASSESS FOR IMMEDIATE REFERRAL–See Home Care*

- any seizure not previously diagnosed
- evidence of injury from seizure
- evidence of alcohol withdrawal

## ASSESS FOR REFERRAL WITHIN 16 HOURS

- diagnosed seizure disorder—notify physician
- child with diagnosed febrile illness, history of febrile seizures, and comfortable caretaker—refer to Fever protocol and notify physician

*Paroxysmal disorder of cerebral function.*

## HOME CARE AND CLIENT TEACHING

### *Instructions for Caregiver*

* protect person from injury
* avoid moving or restraining person unless vomiting occurs
* manage vomiting by supporting person on side to prevent aspiration
* avoid mechanical means of opening airway
* discuss medication instructions with person who has seizure disorder
* instruct person with seizure disorder to avoid driving car or operating machinery until evaluated by physician

## NURSING DIAGNOSES

* anxiety
* breathing pattern, ineffective
* fear
* home maintenance management, impaired
* impaired tissue perfusion, cerebral
* injury, potential for, trauma
* skin integrity, impairment of, potential

# Sexual Assault

 ## ASSESS FOR IMMEDIATE INTERVENTION BY POLICE

- victim calling immediately after assault
- victim not in a safe location

 ## ASSESS FOR IMMEDIATE REFERRAL

- all victims—refer to rape crisis intervention agency
- victim injured in assault—refer to medical facility

 ## CONSIDER FOR ROUTINE APPOINTMENT

- victim calling days or weeks after incident—refer to rape crisis intervention resource or appropriate counselor

▶ ## HOME CARE AND CLIENT TEACHING

*Instructions for Nurse*

- alert callers of the possibility of pregnancy and sexually transmitted disease if they have not undergone medical evaluation after the assault

▶ ## NURSING DIAGNOSES

- anxiety
- comfort, alteration in, pain
- fear
- sexual assault, trauma syndrome, compound reaction
- sexual assault, trauma syndrome, silent reaction
- self-concept, disturbance in, self-esteem
- self-concept, disturbance in, personal identity
- skin integrity, impairment of, potential
- social isolation, potential

# Skin Lesions

## ASSESS FOR IMMEDIATE REFERRAL

- facial swelling with erythema, warmth, and tenderness
- red streak from lesion
- fever over 101° F.

## ASSESS FOR REFERRAL WITHIN 16 HOURS

- lesions surrounded by erythema
- boils
- spreading or enlarging crusted lesions
- children under 1 year of age
- increasing pain
- diabetic

## CONSIDER FOR ROUTINE APPOINTMENT

- genital lesions—consider referral to sexually transmitted disease clinic
- painful lesions on bottom of feet
- wounds not healing properly
- change in appearance of wart, mole, or other lesion
- any lesion not responding to Home Care

*Discrete changes in skin surface.*

## HOME CARE AND CLIENT TEACHING

### *Instructions for Patient*

- treat crusted lesions with soap and water cleaning and anti-biotic ointment four times a day
- maintain good personal hygiene
- consider over-the-counter wart medication for common warts not on feet; use as directed

### *Instructions for Nurse*

- Instruct persons with undiagnosed genital lesions to avoid sexual contact

## NURSING DIAGNOSES

- comfort, alteration in, pain
- home maintenance management, impaired
- injury, potential for, infection
- skin integrity, impairment of, actual

# Sore Throat

 **ASSESS FOR IMMEDIATE REFERRAL**

- sensation of occluding airway
- drooling
- high fever
- profound lethargy
- headache and painful stiff neck
- diabetic with glucose over 300 mg/dl or spilling ketones

 **ASSESS FOR REFERRAL WITHIN 16 HOURS**

- fever
- rash
- swollen glands
- purulent tonsils
- discomfort interfering with fluid intake
- diabetic spilling glucose

 **CONSIDER FOR ROUTINE APPOINTMENT**

- sore throat persisting longer than 3 days

*Pain due to inflammatory process in the pharynx.*

## HOME CARE AND CLIENT TEACHING

*Instructions for Patient*

- rest
- increase intake of liquids
- consider drinking either hot or iced liquids for comfort
- keep humidifier at bedside
- consider aspirin or acetaminophen for discomfort and fever
- gargle with ¼ teaspoon salt in glass of warm water every 2 hours
- try throat lozenges for relief
- consider pet dog as source of recurrent streptococcus infection

## NURSING DIAGNOSES

- breathing pattern, ineffective
- fluid volume deficit, potential
- home maintenance management, impaired

# Spouse Abuse

## ASSESS FOR IMMEDIATE INTERVENTION

- victim in imminent danger—*notify police*
- victim and dependents needing shelter care—*refer to appropriate community resource*

## ASSESS FOR IMMEDIATE REFERRAL

- all victims with injuries—refer to medical facility
- all victims—refer to support group or shelter

## ASSESS FOR REFERRAL WITHIN 16 HOURS TO SUPPORT NETWORK, COUNSELING, OR SHELTER CARE

- victim expressing desperation or fear of abuse
- victim with history of past abuse
- *abuser* seeking counseling or treatment for anger control

*Physical, sexual, or emotional abuse of spouse or partner. Life-threatening injuries—assess acuity by referring to Wounds, Major protocol.*

## ▶ HOME CARE AND CLIENT TEACHING

*Instructions for Nurse*

- reassure callers who are reluctant to seek support or shelter that they can call back

## ▶ NURSING DIAGNOSES

- anxiety
- comfort, alteration in, pain
- coping, ineffective, family, disabling
- coping, ineffective, individual
- fear
- injury, potential for, trauma
- mobility, impaired physical
- self-concept, disturbance in, self-esteem
- skin integrity, impairment of, potential
- violence, potential for

# Stings–Insect & Marine

## ASSESS FOR IMMEDIATE INTERVENTION–See Home Care

- wheezing
- chest tightness
- hives
- facial swelling
- generalized urticaria
- dyspnea

## ASSESS FOR IMMEDIATE REFERRAL–See Home Care

- history of allergic reactions
- multiple stings
- blister on site or purple discoloration of sting
- muscle spasms
- paresthesia
- severe pain

## ASSESS FOR REFERRAL WITHIN 16 HOURS

- signs of infection

## CONSIDER FOR ROUTINE APPOINTMENT

- person in need of tetanus update as indicated by current Immunization Guidelines—see Appendix

*Trauma caused by sting of insect or marine life, such as Portuguese man-of-war or other jellyfish. Stings may or may not be venomous.*

## HOME CARE AND CLIENT TEACHING

*All instructions are for caregiver*

*Insect*

- remove stingers
- apply paste of water and meat tenderizer containing papain to site for 20 minutes, and cover with ice compress
- give injection from bee sting kit to person with emergent symptoms if kit has been prescribed for person
- give oral antihistamine if available and person has taken it before

*Man-of-War or Other Jellyfish*

- apply proximal tourniquet
- wash off tentacles with sea water and a cloth
- neutralize venom with paste of alcohol and meat tenderizer
- remove tourniquet after 1 hour
- loosen tourniquet sooner if circulation becomes impaired
- observe for signs of infection

## NURSING DIAGNOSES

- breathing pattern, ineffective
- cardiac output, alteration in, decreased
- comfort, alteration in, pain
- fear
- gas exchange, impaired
- tissue perfusion, alteration in, cardiopulmonary
- tissue perfusion, alteration in, peripheral

# Suicide, Impending

 **ASSESS FOR IMMEDIATE INTERVENTION**

*Keep person on line and send appropriate help* such as Emergency Medical System personnel, police, or mental health professional.

- person with self-inflicted injury
- person with a specific plan or means and one or more of the following:
    has suffered a recent crisis
    has a debilitating disease
    has a history of suicide attempts or a psychiatric history
    is apparently drunk
    is a parent who has suffered the recent sudden death of a child

---

 **ASSESS FOR IMMEDIATE REFERRAL TO CRISIS LINE**

- person who says, "I cannot go on" but has no specific suicide plan or means
- any severely depressed adolescent, even without suicidal ideation

*Genuine threat of suicide as assessed by nurse.*

## HOME CARE AND CLIENT TEACHING

*Instructions for Nurse*

- reassure caller that a nurse is always available at the number called (or another number), regardless of caller's decision to accept help or not to accept help

## NURSING DIAGNOSES

- coping, ineffective, individual
- fear
- injury, potential for, self-inflicted trauma
- self-concept, disturbance in, personal identity
- self concept, disturbance in, role performance
- self-concept, disturbance in, self-esteem

# Swollen Glands

## ASSESS FOR IMMEDIATE REFERRAL

- dyspnea
- drooling
- difficulty swallowing
- sense of occluding airway

## ASSESS FOR REFERRAL WITHIN 16 HOURS

- fever
- rash
- sore throat
- malaise
- tender or nontender nodes in multiple locations
- swelling larger than size of a marble

## CONSIDER FOR ROUTINE APPOINTMENT

- persistent swelling, either tender or nontender

*Swelling of glands or lymph nodes.*

# HOME CARE AND CLIENT TEACHING

*Instructions for Nurse*

- reassure caller

# NURSING DIAGNOSES

- anxiety
- breathing pattern, ineffective
- comfort, alteration in, pain
- fear

# Syncope

## ASSESS FOR IMMEDIATE INTERVENTION

- diabetic
- chest pain
- inspiratory stridor or other evidence of aspiration
- loss of consciousness lasting longer than 1 minute
- suspicion of trauma or ingestion

## ASSESS FOR IMMEDIATE REFERRAL

- severe or unexplained anxiety
- person under 1 year or over 50 years of age
- localized numbness or weakness
- incontinence
- syncope followed by a period of lethargy or confusion lasting more than a few minutes
- rhythmic jerking lasting more than 10 seconds
- headache
- abdominal pain
- vertigo
- evidence of dehydration

## ASSESS FOR REFERRAL WITHIN 16 HOURS

- toddler with more than three breath-holding incidents in 1 day
- child over 3 years of age with breath-holding behavior

## CONSIDER FOR ROUTINE APPOINTMENT

- repeated syncopal episodes
- repeated breath-holding episodes

*Loss of consciousness lasting less than 1 minute and resolving spontaneously.*

## HOME CARE AND CLIENT TEACHING

*Instructions for Caregiver*

- lay person flat
- remove any noxious stimuli
- consider applying cold compress to forehead and neck
- consider the possibility of pregnancy in woman of childbearing age
- consider the possibility of temper tantrum culminating in breath holding in toddlers:
    observe child
    avoid rescuing child
    avoid giving in to child's request
    reassure child briefly after episode is over
- consider alcohol ingestion as a contributing factor

*Instructions for Nurse*

- reassure everyone involved

## NURSING DIAGNOSES

- anxiety
- coping, ineffective, individual
- fear
- fluid volume deficit, potential
- gas exchange, impaired
- home maintenance management, impaired
- tissue perfusion, alteration in, cardiopulmonary

# Teething

## ASSESS FOR REFERRAL WITHIN 16 HOURS

- lethargy
- high fever

## CONSIDER FOR ROUTINE APPOINTMENT

- irritability not responding to Home Care
- continued drooling
- continued erythematous and swollen gums

*Discomfort and possible complications associated with eruption of new teeth.*

## HOME CARE AND CLIENT TEACHING

### Instructions for Caregiver

- try giving child frozen teething ring, Popsicle, or other frozen object for mouth comfort
- give child prepared teething biscuits
- try over-the-counter topical preparations for gums
- consider acetaminophen drops as needed for discomfort

### Instructions for Nurse

- instruct nursing mother, if she is bitten, to gently remove the nipple from baby's mouth, say "no," and wait a minute before resuming nursing
- reassure caregiver

## NURSING DIAGNOSES

- comfort, alteration in, pain
- oral mucous membrane, alteration in

# Tick Bites

## ASSESS FOR IMMEDIATE REFERRAL

- stiffness, swelling, or pain in joints
- red spot at site of bite expanding to oval rash
- flu-like symptoms 1 to 10 days after tick bite
- fatigue, headache, fever and nausea
- rose-colored spots on hands and feet spreading to entire body
- inability to remove tick at home

*Embedded ticks or bite of one of several species of ticks.*

## HOME CARE AND CLIENT TEACHING

### Instructions for Patient

- prevent tick bites with repellent containing permethrin, if available; otherwise, use another insect repellent
- conduct frequent inspections of skin and scalp when hiking, camping, or picnicking
- remove tick *carefully* by covering with petroleum jelly, forcing tick to let go for air
- disinfect bite with soap and water and antiseptic

## NURSING DIAGNOSES

- home maintenance management, impaired
- injury, potential for, infection
- skin integrity, impairment of, actual

# Unresponsiveness

 **ASSESS FOR IMMEDIATE INTERVENTION–See Home Care**

- any person unresponsive longer than 1 minute

*Complete unresponsiveness to vigorous shaking and shouting.*

## HOME CARE AND CLIENT TEACHING

### *Instructions for Caregiver*

- *do not move* if injury is suspected
- maintain patent airway as directed by current American Heart Association guidelines
- check identification for evidence of diabetes or other chronic illness
- ventilate enclosed spaces
- obtain evidence of drugs or toxins ingested and bring to medical facility
- remove wet clothing and cover with warm blankets if exposure to cold is suspected
- remove clothing and apply cool, wet compresses if heat exposure is suspected

## NURSING DIAGNOSES

- airway clearance, ineffective
- gas exchange, impaired
- tissue perfusion, alteration in, cardiopulmonary
- tissue perfusion, alteration in, cerebral

# Urinary Discomfort

## ASSESS FOR IMMEDIATE REFERRAL

- fever over 101° F.
- vomiting
- diabetic
- acute flank or abdominal pain
- acute urinary retention

## ASSESS FOR REFERRAL WITHIN 16 HOURS

- urinary frequency with thirst and weight loss
- dysuria
- hematuria
- urinary frequency and urgency
- pain following ejaculation
- urethral discharge
- perineal pain

## CONSIDER FOR ROUTINE APPOINTMENT

- incontinence

*Discomfort associated with urination.*

## ▶ HOME CARE AND CLIENT TEACHING

### *Instructions for Patient*

- increase liquid intake to 16 glasses a day
- increase intake of cranberry juice
- try sitting in warm bath to void four times a day to ease discomfort with voiding
- consider medications as possible contributors to urinary retention

### *Instructions for Nurse*

- consider referral to sexually transmitted disease clinic

## ▶ NURSING DIAGNOSES

- anxiety
- comfort, alteration in, pain
- fluid volume deficit, potential
- home maintenance management, impaired
- tissue perfusion, alteration in, renal
- urinary elimination, alteration in, patterns

# Vaginal Bleeding

 **ASSESS FOR IMMEDIATE REFERRAL**

- saturation of more than 4 tampons or pads per hour
- saturation of more than 1 tampon or pad per hour for 6 hours
- severe pain
- fever
- rapid pulse
- dizziness, lightheadedness, or syncope
- prepubescent
- flow heavier than normal menstrual period during first trimester of pregnancy or after a missed period
- bright red bleeding during second or third trimester
- trauma
- recent pelvic surgery
- recent delivery

 **ASSESS FOR REFERRAL WITHIN 16 HOURS**

- spotting after missed period or during first trimester of pregnancy—notify physician

 **CONSIDER FOR ROUTINE APPOINTMENT**

- heavy menstrual bleeding
- repeated midcycle bleeding
- postmenopausal bleeding

## HOME CARE AND CLIENT TEACHING

### *Instructions for Patient*

- treat spotting or light bleeding with rest
- consider acetaminophen for minor discomfort
- consider the possibility of pregnancy if menstrual period has been missed or flow has decreased suddenly

### *Instructions for Nurse*

- reassure caretaker of newborn that small amount of spotting on diaper is not dangerous

## NURSING DIAGNOSES

- anxiety
- cardiac output, alteration in, decreased
- fear
- fluid volume deficit, potential
- home maintenance management, impaired
- tissue perfusion, alteration in, reproductive

# Vaginal Discharge & Itching

## ASSESS FOR IMMEDIATE REFERRAL

- pelvic pain
- sexual assault victim

## ASSESS FOR REFERRAL WITHIN 16 HOURS

- urinary frequency
- diabetic
- pregnant woman
- foul-smelling discharge
- discomfort
- prepubescent
- suspected exposure to sexually transmitted disease—consider referral to sexually transmitted disease clinic

## CONSIDER FOR ROUTINE APPOINTMENT

- recurrent discharge
- discharge or itching unrelieved by Home Care

## HOME CARE AND CLIENT TEACHING

*Instructions for Patient*

- avoid wearing panty hose
- wear cotton panties
- apply cold compresses to vulva b.i.d.
- avoid colored and scented toilet paper
- avoid feminine hygiene deodorant products
- avoid deodorant tampons
- consider possible sensitivity to soap, douche, or clothing
- decrease intake of sugar
- consider antibiotic use, pregnancy, or diabetes as possible cause
- try drinking acidophilus milk and eating yogurt with live cultures for recurrent yeast infections

*Instructions for Nurse*

- suggest douching once with 1 tablespoon of vinegar in 1 quart warm water, followed by douching b.i.d. with 3 ounces of yogurt well mixed in 1 quart warm water for 2 days; suggest only if woman is confident she has yeast infection and seems competent and reliable
- reassure caretaker of newborn that small amount of spotting on diaper is not dangerous
- instruct caller not to douche within 48 hours of medical appointment

## NURSING DIAGNOSES

- comfort, alteration in, pain
- injury, potential for, infection

# Visual Disturbances

## ASSESS FOR IMMEDIATE REFERRAL—See Home Care

- injury to head, face, or eye
- sudden onset of diplopia, shadow, or flap in visual field, or a visual deficit
- third trimester of pregnancy
- pain
- misshapen iris
- nausea and vomiting

## ASSESS FOR REFERRAL WITHIN 16 HOURS

- disturbance present longer than 72 hours
- diabetic
- floaters

## CONSIDER FOR ROUTINE APPOINTMENT

- intermittent visual deficit not present at time of call
- slowly increasing visual deficit

*Alteration of normal vision.*

## HOME CARE AND CLIENT TEACHING

*Instructions for Nurse*

- reassure caller

## NURSING DIAGNOSES

- comfort, alteration in, pain
- sensory perception alteration, visual

# Vomiting—Adult

## ASSESS FOR IMMEDIATE REFERRAL

- severe headache not previously diagnosed
- severe abdominal pain
- hematemesis
- profound, unexplained fear
- vomiting preceded by head injury
- stiff neck
- decreased level of consciousness
- syncope
- diabetic unable to retain adequate fluids and carbohydrates
- ileostomy

## ASSESS FOR REFERRAL WITHIN 16 HOURS

- diabetic—see Home Care*
- pregnant woman with severe vomiting
- fever
- unresponsive to Home Care
- previously diagnosed severe headache

## CONSIDER FOR ROUTINE APPOINTMENT

- annoying, mild vomiting during pregnancy
- intermittent vomiting
- habit of gorging and vomiting with overconcern about weight

*Forceful emptying of stomach contents orally.*

## HOME CARE AND CLIENT TEACHING

### Instructions for Caregiver

* consider treating diabetics at home for up to 15 hours if they can retain 10 grams carbohydrates every hour; 10 grams equals one of the following:
    ½ cup soda pop, lemonade, or Kool-aid
    1 cup Gatorade
    ¼ Popsicle
    2 teaspoons syrup, honey, jelly, or sugar
    ¼ cup Jello
    4 saltine crackers
    5 Lifesavers

### Instructions for Patient

● *test urine or blood for glucose and ketones every 4 hours if diabetic*
● try frequent, small amounts of food for mild symptoms
● observe the following dietary guidelines:
    N.P.O. for 4 hours after vomiting,
    then sip on clear liquids for 24 hours, and
    finally proceed to soft diet

## NURSING DIAGNOSES

● anxiety
● comfort, alteration in, pain
● fluid volume deficit, potential
● home maintenance management, impaired
● tissue perfusion, alteration in, gastrointestinal

# Vomiting–Pediatric

## ASSESS FOR IMMEDIATE REFERRAL

- extremely anxious parent
- vomiting of blood or "coffee ground" material
- abdominal pain other than just before vomiting with relief after vomiting
- diabetic
- vomiting preceded by viral infection or chicken pox 4 to 6 days earlier
- lethargy or disorientation and agitation
- rapid or labored breathing
- decreasing urine output
- no tears with crying and dry mouth and lips
- vomiting preceded by abdominal injury
- vomiting preceded by head injury
- urinary tract symptoms
- ear pain or pulling at ears
- projectile vomiting in infant less than 6 months of age
- inability to take prescribed medications
- fever over 101° F.
- stiff neck
- possible ingestion of toxic plant, drug, or chemical
- suspected medication reaction
- infant less than 6 months of age with diarrhea

## ASSESS FOR REFERRAL WITHIN *8* HOURS

- unresponsive to Home Care

## CONSIDER FOR ROUTINE APPOINTMENT

- periodic, recurrent episodes of vomiting
- concern about infant spitting up

*Forceful emptying of stomach contents orally in a child.*

▶ ## HOME CARE AND CLIENT TEACHING

### *Instructions for Caregiver*

- try this dietary regimen:
  give 1 tablespoon clear liquids every 20 minutes for 1 hour; if no vomiting occurs, gradually increase amount until child is drinking normally; proceed to soft diet for 24 hours, and then proceed to normal diet
- consider giving an oral electrolyte maintenance solution such as Pedialyte or Infalyte to child under 1 year and diluted Gatorade to child over 1 year
- continue breast feeding

### *Instructions for Nurse*

- reassure caregiver of infant who is spitting up, and encourage increased burping

▶ ## NURSING DIAGNOSES

- anxiety
- comfort, alteration in, pain
- fluid volume deficit, potential
- nutrition, alteration in, less than body requirements

# Weight Loss

### ASSESS FOR IMMEDIATE REFERRAL

- children with vomiting or diarrhea resulting in weight loss of more than 5% of normal weight
- elderly or debilitated person with vomiting or diarrhea resulting in weight loss

### ASSESS FOR REFERRAL WITHIN 16 HOURS

- chronic and acute weight loss with overconcern about weight
- increased thirst and urination

### CONSIDER FOR ROUTINE APPOINTMENT

- chronic or acute weight loss unresponsive to Home Care
- weight loss of more than 10 pounds not related to dieting

*Inability to maintain normal weight.*

## HOME CARE AND CLIENT TEACHING

### *Instructions for Patient*

- consider supplemental feedings of high calorie, highly nutritious foods such as milk shakes or processed nutritional supplements

## NURSING DIAGNOSES

- anxiety
- fluid volume deficit, potential
- home maintenance management, impaired
- nutrition, alteration in, less than body requirements

# Wheezing

### ASSESS FOR IMMEDIATE INTERVENTION

- fear of impending respiratory arrest
- cyanosis
- sudden onset after exposure to known antigen
- sudden onset after possible foreign body aspiration
- rapid respiratory rate
- extreme anxiety

### ASSESS FOR IMMEDIATE REFERRAL

- exhaustion
- any wheezing not listed elsewhere in protocol

### ASSESS FOR REFERRAL WITHIN 16 HOURS

- previously diagnosed wheezing that is not severe and not worsening at time of call

### CONSIDER FOR ROUTINE APPOINTMENT

- intermittent wheezing not present at time of call

*Lower airway obstruction characterized by prolonged expiratory sound.*

---

## ▶ HOME CARE AND CLIENT TEACHING

### *Instructions to Patient*

- encourage increased intake of clear liquids
- take medicine as prescribed by physician
- consider using humidifier
- consider maintaining a log of episodes to discover precipitating factors
- avoid exposure to known allergens

### *Instructions to Caregiver*

- calm anxious child

### *Instructions to Nurse*

- reassure caregiver

---

## ▶ NURSING DIAGNOSES

- airway clearance, ineffective
- breathing pattern, ineffective
- fear
- fluid volume deficit, potential
- gas exchange, impaired
- home maintenance management, impaired
- tissue perfusion, alteration in, cardiopulmonary

# Wounds, Major

**ASSESS FOR IMMEDIATE INTERVENTION—See Home Care**

- object impaled in wound
- penetrating chest, back, or abdominal wounds
- neck injury
- back injury
- blunt trauma to chest, back, or abdomen
- extremity amputation—see Home Care*
- extremity deformity
- blow to head or face resulting in loss of consciousness
- bleeding not controlled by direct pressure
- crush injury to torso
- extensive second- or third-degree burns

*Major injury to skin or underlying tissue or organs.*

## HOME CARE AND CLIENT TEACHING

*Instructions for Caregiver*

* care for amputated part by placing it in a plastic bag, sealing the bag, then placing it in a container of ice water
● avoid moving injured person
● stop bleeding by direct pressure with hand and heavy cloth
● cover person with blankets
● cover chest wounds
● cover open wounds in deformed extremities
● avoid removing impaled objects

## NURSING DIAGNOSES

● breathing pattern, ineffective
● comfort, alteration in, pain
● fluid volume deficit, potential
● gas exchange, impaired
● injury, potential for, paralysis
● skin integrity, impairment of, actual
● tissue perfusion, alteration in, cardiopulmonary
● tissue perfusion, alteration in, gastrointestinal
● tissue perfusion, alteration in, peripheral
● tissue perfusion, alteration in, renal

# Wounds, Minor

## ASSESS FOR IMMEDIATE REFERRAL

- uncontrolled bleeding—see Home Care*
- lacerations on face, hands, feet, chest, abdomen, back, scalp, or joints
- lacerations larger than ½ inch across
- human bites
- loss of function
- protruding tissue
- lip wounds through vermilion border
- embedded dirt or foreign body
- extreme tenderness
- dirty puncture wounds including those made through a shoe
- wounds caused by projectiles
- bleeding over site of extreme tenderness

## ASSESS FOR REFERRAL WITHIN 16 HOURS

- redness, swelling, or increased tenderness

## CONSIDER FOR ROUTINE APPOINTMENT

- person in need of tetanus update as indicated by current Immunization Guidelines—see Appendix
- lesions not healed after 2 weeks of Home Care

*Traumatic disruption of skin integrity.*

# HOME CARE AND CLIENT TEACHING

### *Instructions for Caregiver*

* apply direct pressure with clean, dry cloth for 20 minutes or until bleeding has stopped; then cover
* clean thoroughly with warm, soapy water, and cover with clean, dry cloth
* clean unsutured wounds t.i.d. with warm, soapy water; then consider application of antibiotic ointment
* soak puncture wounds in warm, soapy water t.i.d. until healed
* use good oral hygiene t.i.d.; use saline or dilute hydrogen peroxide rinses for mouth and lip wounds
* watch carefully for signs of infection

### *Instructions for Nurse*

* caution diabetics about increased risk of infection and the need for meticulous hygiene and observation

# NURSING DIAGNOSES

* comfort, alteration in, pain
* fluid volume deficit, potential
* home maintenance management, impaired
* skin integrity, impairment of, actual
* tissue perfusion, alteration in, peripheral

# IMMUNIZATION GUIDELINES

This appendix provides current guidelines for immunization with the most common vaccines and anticipated reactions to those immunizations. It is limited to routine immunization for health maintenance. Complete immunization information, including travel and occupational considerations, can be obtained from the Public Health Service Division of the U.S. Department of Health and Human Services.

This is a tool for caller education, not assessment. Assess signs of illness and triage with the appropriate protocol.

Encourage callers to maintain immunization records for themselves and children in their care.

| Immunization* | Recommended for | Schedule | Common Reactions |
|---|---|---|---|
| • Diphtheria and tetanus toxoids | • Persons over age 6 | • Initial series: Two injections 4 weeks apart Third in 6 to 12 months<br>• Booster at age 14 to 16 and every 10 years thereafter | • Injection site redness, swelling, and tenderness lasting up to a week<br>• Fever<br>• Malaise |
| • Diphtheria and tetanus toxoids and pertussis vaccine | • Children aged 2 months to 6 years | • Three injections at least 6 weeks apart beginning at age 2 months<br>• Booster at age 15 months<br>• Booster before starting school | • Injection site redness and tenderness<br>• Moderate fever beginning within 24 hours of injection and lasting 24 hours or less<br>• Occasional fever<br>• Injection site redness and swelling |
| • Haemophilus b conjugate vaccine | • Children aged 18 months to 5 years | • One injection | • Rare allergic reactions |

(*continued on next page*)

| Immunization* | Recommended for | Schedule | Common Reactions |
|---|---|---|---|
| • Hepatitis B virus vaccine | • Homosexual males<br>• Users of illicit injectable drugs<br>• Household members and sexual contacts of hepatitis B carriers<br>• Residents and staff of institutions for the developmentally disabled<br>• Hemodialysis patients<br>• Recipients of coagulation Factor VIII or IX<br>• Morticians<br>• Prostitutes<br>• Dentists and dental hygienists<br>• Health care workers who are frequently in contact with blood | • Two injections 1 month apart<br>Third injection 5 months later | • None |
| • Influenza virus vaccine | • Persons aged 65 and over<br>• Persons with chronic pulmonary, cardiovascular, metabolic, or renal disease; severe anemia; or compromised immune function<br>• Health care workers who are in contact with high risk patients | • One injection annually | • Injection site tenderness<br>• Fever of short duration<br>• Malaise of short duration |
| • Measles virus vaccine, live attenuated | • Persons born after 1956 without a history of previous immunizations at age 1 or older and without laboratory evidence of immunity | • One injection | • Fever<br>• Minimal rash during month following injection |
| • Measles, mumps, and rubella vaccine, live | • Children aged 15 months to puberty | • One injection | • Moderate fever 5 to 12 days after injection<br>• Mild rash, malaise, and transient joint pain during month following injection |
| • Pneumococcal vaccine | • Persons aged 65 and over<br>• Persons over age 2 with cardiovascular or pulmonary disease, Hodgkin's disease, splenic dysfunction, asplenia, renal failure, cirrhosis, alcoholism, multiple myeloma, cerebrospinal fluid leaks, or compromised immune function | • One injection | • Erythema and soreness at injection site lasting up to 48 hours<br>• Low grade fever occurring within 24 hours and lasting 24 hours or less |

| Immunization* | Recommended for | Schedule | Common Reactions |
|---|---|---|---|
| • Poliovirus vaccine, live oral | • Children; polio vaccine is not normally recommended for adults | • Two doses at least 6 weeks apart<br>• Additional doses at 15 months of age and before starting school | • None |
| • Rubella virus vaccine, live | • Nonpregnant women of childbearing age without laboratory evidence of immunity. Pregnancy should be avoided for 3 months after receiving vaccine. | • One injection | • Sore throat<br>• Malaise<br>• Injection site tenderness<br>• Mild joint pain, either transient or long term |
| • Tetanus toxoid | • Persons with skin-penetrating injury who have had no tetanus immunization within the previous 5 to 10 years | • One injection every 5 to 10 years | • Fever<br>• Injection site redness, sweling, and tenderness lasting up to a week<br>• Malaise |

*Guidelines may vary for persons who test HIV positive.

# Index

Note: Page numbers in *italics* refer to illustrations; page numbers followed by (t) refer to tables.